Colorado

AMERICA THE BEAUTIFUL

Colorado

Jean F. Blashfield

Children's Press®
A Division of Scholastic Inc.
New York Toronto London Auckland Sydney
Mexico City New Delhi Hong Kong
Danbury, Connecticut

Frontispiece: **San Juan Mountains**

Front cover: **Mount Owen, in the Sangre de Cristo Mountains**

Back cover: **The Denver skyline**

Consultant: Karen Zoltenko, Colorado State Archives

Please note: All statistics are as up-to-date as possible at the time of publication.

Book production by Editorial Directions, Inc.

Library of Congress Cataloging-in-Publication Data

Blashfield, Jean F.
Colorado / Jean F. Blashfield.
144 p. 24 cm. — (America the beautiful. Second series)
Includes bibliographical references and index.
Summary : Describes the geography, plants and animals, history, economy, language, religions, cultures, sports and arts, and people of the state of Colorado.
ISBN 0-516-20684-2
1. Colorado—Juvenile literature. [1. Colorado.] I. Title. II. Series.
F776.3.B53 1999
917.88—dc21 96-19855
CIP
AC

Printed in the United States of America
5 6 7 8 9 0 R 08 07 06 05

Acknowledgments

Like all writers, I am totally indebted to librarians. They are the people who treasure information, delight in organizing it, relish confirming it, and rejoice in sharing it. My special thanks for assistance in preparing this book go to: The Denver Public Library; The State Historical Society of Colorado; the Colorado State Archives; the Hedburg Public Library, Janesville; the Wisconsin University of Wisconsin—Madison; the Memorial Library (and their fine catalog on the Internet); and the State Historical Society of Wisconsin. And thanks to The Broadmoor, Colorado Springs, for being there for honeymoons.

Pikes Peak

Colorado River

Aspen

Contents

Snowboarding

Downhill skiing

Denver

Near Piney Lake

Bighorn sheep

CHAPTER ONE

Colorado Inspiration

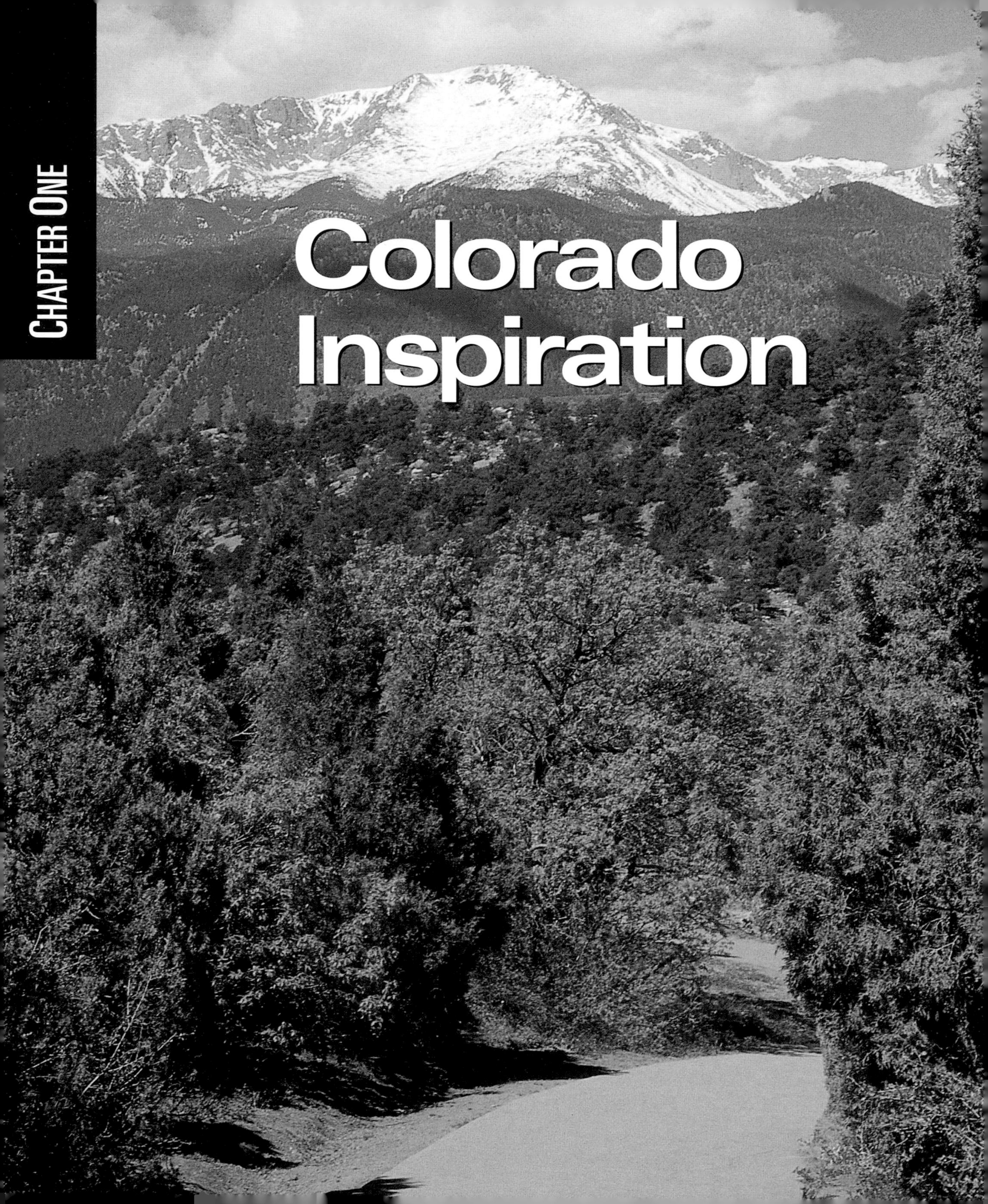

Katharine Lee Bates was inspired to write "America the Beautiful" after seeing Pikes Peak.

Katharine Lee Bates was a Massachusetts professor and poet who spent the summer of 1893 teaching at Colorado College in Colorado Springs. She and her friends made a trip up Pikes Peak one summer day. She stood at the top and looked out over Colorado's fertile plains to the east. As she turned first to the north, then west and south, all about her were spectacular mountains, with peak after peak piercing the spacious skies.

Awestruck, she felt the words "America the beautiful" come into her mind. The image stayed with her as she returned to the college, and soon those words became the title of a new poem. In the poem, she prayed that the beauty and majesty she had seen from Pikes Peak should be "undimmed by human tears" and that brotherhood would come to all "from sea to shining sea."

Soon published, Bates's poem was immediately popular. Set to music by Samuel A. Ward, "America the Beautiful" has become one of America's most beloved songs. No one who lives in or visits Colorado ever quite forgets the words. Her prayer in the poem is reflected in the state's motto: *Nil sine Numine,* which means "Nothing without Providence."

A Quick Look at the Centennial State

Beneath the awesome beauty that so inspired Katharine Lee Bates live the people of Colorado. Like people everywhere, they go to school, raise their children, enjoy their neighborhoods, reflect on

Opposite: The breathtaking view of Pikes Peak has brought many visitors to Colorado.

their history, decide elections, hunt for jobs, and plan for the future.

Colorado had been a state less than twenty years when Bates visited Colorado Springs. The state's shape had been defined in 1861 when it was declared a territory.

Colorado is one of the few states that has none of its boundaries with other states defined by a natural structure—a river, a range of

A Colorado ecology club studying the San Juan Mountains region

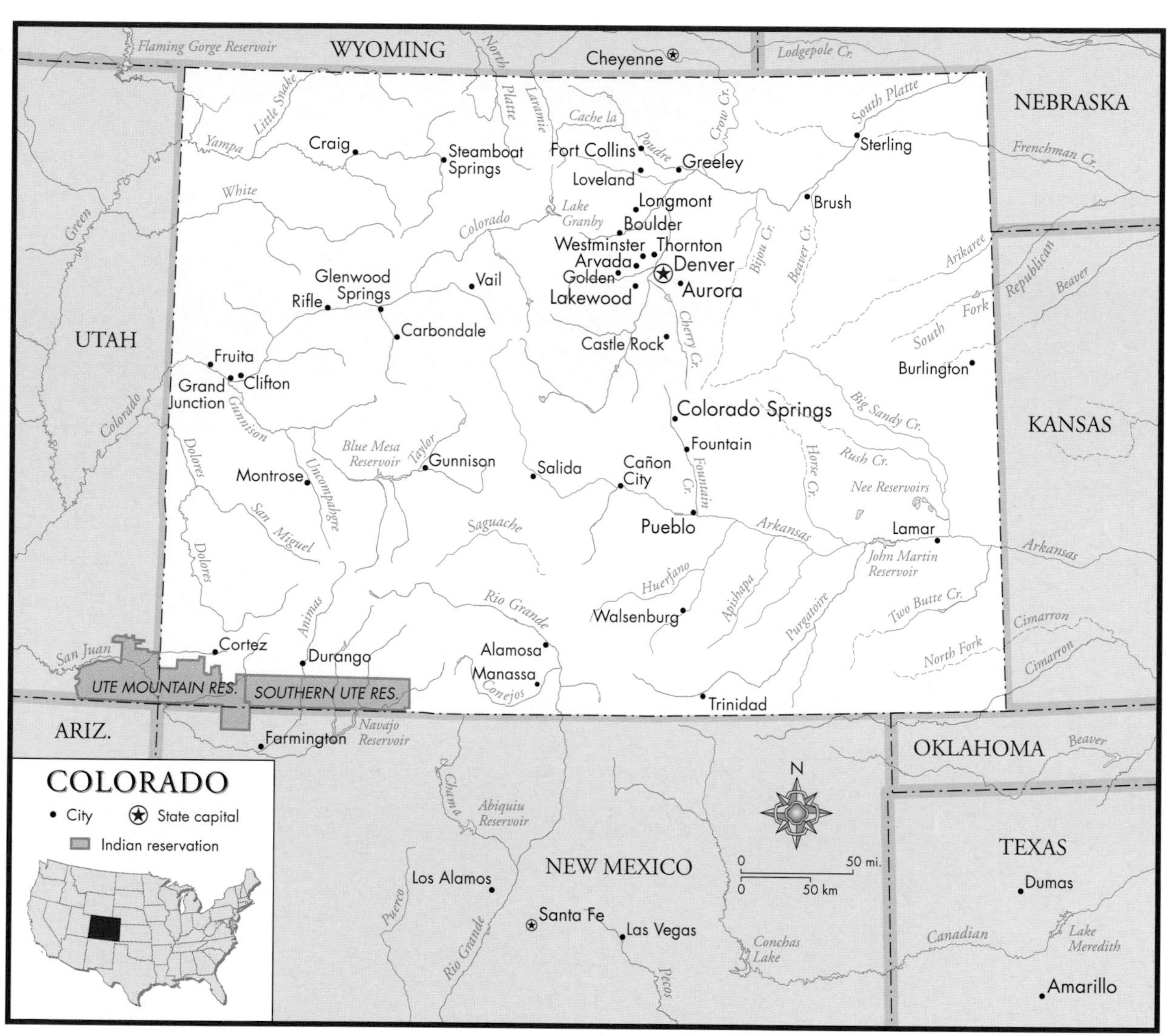

hills, a coast. Its boundaries are defined strictly as lines of latitude and longitude on a map. It seems as if that should make the state completely rectangular; but its 275-mile (443-km) distance from north to south is enough to make the northern boundary slightly shorter than the southern.

Geopolitical map of Colorado

The Four Corners region in the southwestern corner of the state is the only place in the United States where four states meet. If you're agile enough, you can stand at that place (which is marked by a metal plaque), lean over, and put each hand and foot in a different state—Colorado, Utah, New Mexico, and Arizona.

Seventeen different flags of nations and U.S. territories have flown over the land that is now Colorado. After 1861, only one flag remained, the U.S. flag. Fifteen years later, it became the thirty-eighth state. It was called the Centennial State because it became a state on August 1, 1876, the year of the centennial—or one-hundredth anniversary—of the nation.

Colorado's name means "red-colored" in Spanish. It was taken from the name of its major river, which has water colored by the red sandstone through which it runs. The state lies nearly in the middle of the United States. It's also right in the middle in population—twenty-fourth with just over 4 million people. By area, Colorado ranks eighth, with 104,100 square miles (269,618 sq km). As a whole, Colorado has 41 people per square mile (16 people per sq km). Only eleven states have a lower population density. Almost half of Colorado's people live in the Denver area, but the remainder of Colorado has plenty of the wide open spaces that Katharine Lee Bates would recognize.

Opposite: The Colorado River was named for its red appearance.

Chapter Two

Mesas and Miners

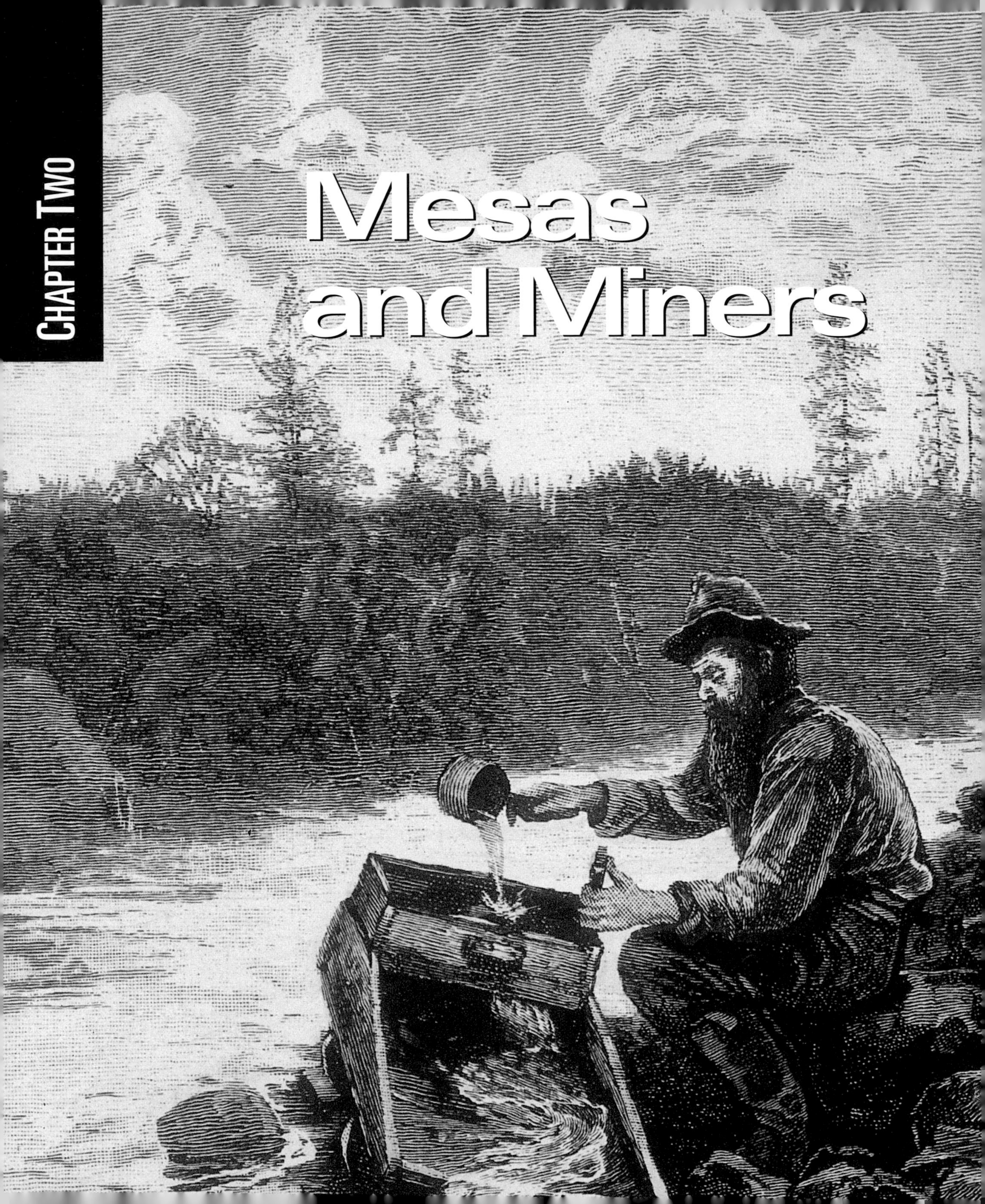

The first traces of human life in the region that became Colorado are stone objects that were shaped into tools. Found in Weld County, these flint points have been determined to be at least 12,000 years old. The people who left them probably came from the south. They entered the area chasing the prehistoric elephants called mammoths and mastodons. In later centuries, these gigantic animals disappeared, but hunters still came in pursuit of bison and other game.

The Anasazi lived among Colorado's cliffs.

Between 5000 and 1000 B.C., various peoples farmed along the river valleys of eastern Colorado. They probaby brought their agricultural techniques with them from the Great Plains farther east.

The first human inhabitants of Colorado about whom we know much have been called the Basket Makers. They occupied the mesas (flat-topped mountains) of southwestern Colorado before A.D. 100. They are known mainly by the clay containers they left behind. They used the containers to store water and some corn.

Several hundred years later, a different group took over the Basket Makers' land. They may have taken it by war, or the two groups may have merged. By A.D. 700, however, these people, who are now called Pre-Pueblos, were living on the land. Then, about three hundred years later, their sites were taken over by the pueblo-builders, whose cliff dwellings are still seen today.

Opposite: The Gold Rush in Colorado

The Anasazi

These people who built cliff dwellings are now called the Anasazi, or "ancient ones." They built great cities, or pueblos, that trail down the steep sides of the mesas. They built houses, official buildings, grain storehouses, and apartment houses of several stories. They quarried stone for their buildings and cut down trees many miles around to use in making roofs. They dug huge ceremonial chambers deep into the cliff tops.

On the mesa tops as well as down on the floors of the canyons below, the Anasazi planted corn, or maize. It grew because they used every means possible to capture the rain that fell, even though it didn't rain very often. They built dams that collected water in small reservoirs to hold it until it rained again. The region had occasional short periods of drought that the Indians could prepare for. Nothing could have prepared them, though, for the great drought that lasted at least twenty-five years beginning in the year 1276. That date has been identified from the annual rings of trees that grew in the area.

Without rain, the people could not grow corn. Without corn, they could not survive in the homeland they had known for so long. For two decades, they tried to hang on. Finally, they gave up and began to abandon their cities in an orderly way.

Today, we don't know for sure where those early Native Americans went, but the structures they left behind were preserved by the dry air of the high land in the Four Corners regions. The largest is called Cliff Palace. It has been dated to about 1175. Built under the roof of a gigantic open cave, Cliff Palace contains 217 rooms, plus 23 kivas (underground ceremonial chambers). It was the first structure found by Europeans in what became Mesa Verde National Park.

Tribal People

The people called Utes came into the river valleys of western Colorado to spend the winters but spread throughout the area during the summers. The Ute people spoke Shoshone and occupied open lands on the mountains. In fact, their name, *Ute*, means "people who dwell in the tops of mountains." They were able to protect their homes just by blocking the passes through the mountains. The Plains people usually did not even try to enter Ute territory.

The Utes have inhabited Colorado longer than any other people. They lived on the plentiful game found on the mountain slopes, the fish in the tumbling streams, and the berries and fruits that grew naturally.

Apache, Navajo, and various similar peoples came down from Canada, speaking quite different Athabaskan languages. They occupied the plains in eastern Colorado.

Colorow, a Ute chief

Visitors from South and East

That is how things stood in Colorado in 1540. That year, Spaniard Francisco Vásquez de Coronado, governor of a province in Mexico, led an expedition northward to search for the legendary "Seven Golden Cities of Cibola." But the "cities" they found were sad little pueblo villages, and there was no gold. The strength of the rumors about gold led Coronado to send one of his lieutenants, Garcia López de Cárdenas, to investigate farther. He and his men found the Grand Canyon on the Colorado River, but, again, no

Coronado led a 1540 march through what is now Colorado.

gold. However, Coronado's expedition gave Spain a claim to the vast lands of the American Southwest.

Two years later, Coronado led another expedition in which the men saw small villages along the river they were calling Rio Grande. Reports of these villages prompted Mexico to send missionaries northward. In 1598, Juan de Oñate headed an expedition to establish a colony called New Mexico. Its purpose was to convert the Indian people of the area—whether they wanted to be converted or not. For the next hundred years, Mexico's influence was quite local—except in one way.

The Horse and New Tribes

The major effect the Spanish had on people living in Colorado was that Spanish horses were allowed to run wild and began to populate the Southwest. At first, the Native Americans called the horse "mystery dog," and they used it for food. Soon they found, though,

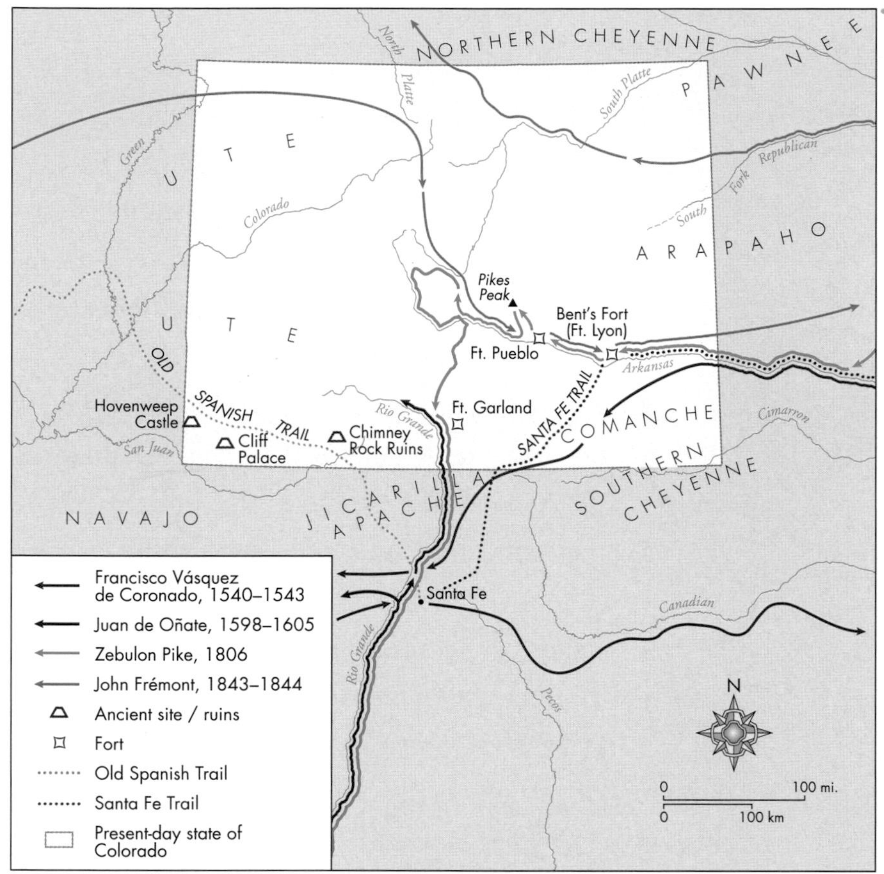

Exploration of Colorado

that the mystery dogs could be ridden, which enabled them to make war on neighboring tribes.

Farming tribes quickly became hunting tribes because on horses they could chase the bison that roamed the plains of eastern Colorado. The Utes abandoned their mountains and also became bison hunters.

The Comanche of Colorado and northern New Mexico had been a fairly insignificant tribe until they acquired horses from the Spanish. Then they became famed and feared for their riding skills. They began to count their wealth in terms of horses, which were particularly useful in stealing territory from the Jicarilla Apache.

The Comanche became stronger when they acquired horses from the Spaniards.

The Jicarilla Apache were also enemies of the Utes, who gave them the name "Apache," which comes from a Ute word meaning "enemies" or "those who fight me." The Comanche controlled the plains and the bison in Colorado for decades.

In 1706, an expedition from New Mexico entered the Arkansas River Valley. Juan de Ulibarri and his soldiers explored the region centered around what is now the city of Pueblo. There were many small tribal villages along the river. Ulibarri claimed the region, which he called San Luis, for Spain.

The Spanish in Mexico mostly ignored their new "province," especially after a large group of Spanish soldiers were killed by the Pawnee in western Nebraska. French traders and trappers entered the area in search of good furs, but the Native Americans ignored them because their numbers were so small. They were more concerned about the growing Spanish settlements in nearby New Mexico.

From safety in Colorado, the Comanche carried out numerous raids into New Mexico. In 1779, the Spanish had had enough of their deadly harassment. They sent Juan Bautista de Anza (an officer who had founded San Francisco in California) into Colorado to take on the Comanche. Anza gathered Utes as his allies, and together, they turned on the Comanche, eventually killing many important warriors.

The Comanche moved southward, and other tribes of Native Americans began to arrive in Colorado. The Cheyenne and the Arapaho arrived from the Dakotas, hoping to find horses and bison. They found both, but they also found a growing stream of white people arriving from the East.

Two Nations in One State

The Spanish never actually drew a border and said "this is our land." Even if they had, the border would have changed regularly as the French moved in and out. The boundaries did not become more definite until 1803, when France sold the Louisiana Territory to the young United States.

In 1806, Zebulon Pike and twenty-two other men set out from Missouri to explore north and west. Their mission was to find the source of the Arkansas River and the Red River (not realizing that the Red River is in Texas). They had been on the move for four months when they caught their first sight of the Rocky Mountains. One single peak of incredible height, which they could see from 150 miles (241 km) away, Pike later reported to be unclimbable. It was given his name.

Zebulon Pike

An 1819 treaty with Spain set the boundary between Spanish and U.S. territory through Colorado, along the Arkansas River. Mexico acquired its independence from Spain and opened up New Mexico to trade. Traders from the United States began to create a new trail to Santa Fe, New Mexico. In Colorado, the Santa Fe Trail ran beside the Arkansas River, and it was there that the enterprising Bent brothers set up business as traders.

The Bents and Their Fort

William and Charles Bent and their partner, Ceran St. Vrain, owned a major trading company through which they focused development in the Old West. On the Santa Fe Trail, by the Arkansas River, the three men built an adobe "castle" in 1833. It was intended to house travelers and to serve as a trading post for the fur trade. They bought beaver and buffalo pelts from trappers and Native Americans and then shipped them by wagon train to St. Louis, Missouri. For the wagon trains that had spent weeks crossing the Great Plains, the sight of Bent's Fort was a great relief.

William Bent, a native of St. Louis, married Owl Woman, a Cheyenne woman, and often played an influential role in keeping peace between the white people and the Cheyenne. He is generally recognized as the first white settler in Colorado. The famed Kit Carson served as a hunter for Bent's Fort.

During the Mexican War of 1846, U.S. soldiers stripped Bent's Fort of all it had, and though he was promised payment from the U.S. government, Bent never received it. Rather than let Bent's Fort go to the federal government without full payment, William Bent placed kegs of gunpowder around the fort walls and deliberately destroyed most of the spectacular building. ■

The Mexican Years

Mexico began to concern itself with the lands it owned far to the north after 1836, when Texas became an independent republic. Fearing that it might lose control of those northern lands, the Mexican government made grants of large estates in the San Luis Valley. The settlers were mostly mestizos, people of mixed Spanish and Indian ancestry.

After Mexico lost the Mexican War of 1846, all its lands north of the Rio Grande were ceded to the United States. The U.S. government agreed to leave the Mexicans who were living in those northern regions alone, but it did not keep its word. It did not prevent emigrants from moving from New Mexico into Colorado.

In 1854, on Christmas Day, the Utes, angry at seeing more and more settlers come into the San Luis Valley, killed fifteen men at Fort Pueblo. Within a few months, U.S. soldiers had subdued them. Thirty years later, these Native Americans would make one last try.

A Colorado Gold Rush settlement in 1859

The Gold Rush

Gold was discovered in California in 1848. The gold seekers who rushed past Colorado did not even pause to admire its beautiful mountains. Not all of those prospectors found gold, however. Some of the discouraged men headed back east and, this time, were drawn to the Rocky Mountains.

In the spring and summer of 1858, Green Russell and a group of avid prospectors were panning for gold in Cherry Creek, a tributary of the South Platte River in what would later be the suburbs of Denver. To pan, they scooped pans with screen bottoms into the waters of the creek. The holes in the screen were large enough to let sand fall through but small enough to stop any flakes of gold large enough to have value. Gold deposits where prospectors can wash flakes or nuggets out of sand and water are called placer mines.

In the East, a major economic depression was under way. Many people were finding it hard to make a living. In addition, from Kansas eastward, the people were increasingly aware that a civil war was brewing. When the news that gold had been discovered in Colorado hit the East, thousands of people headed toward the mountains.

Making Towns

Very little gold was found that first year, and most would-be miners at Cherry Creek gave up. Nevertheless, the villages of tents and lean-tos made out of pine boughs they had built were there to stay. Two of the villages merged and became Denver. It was said that during some weeks five thousand hopeful men arrived in Colorado's Front Range.

Those people who became discouraged about mining often established businesses in support of the miners, or they began to farm, just as they had back in the East. These were the mountain area's first real settlers.

A prospector named Abe Lee found some gold nuggets in the water at the bottom of California Gulch, some miles west of Denver, in 1860. He couldn't keep his news quiet, and within weeks, Oro City got its start. Other mountain communities such as Central City and Black Hawk in Gregory Gulch started in the same way. Such towns were not temporary collections of shacks. Within no more than five years, one visitor described them as "thriving, orderly, peaceable, busy . . . with churches and schools."

The mining towns, like towns anywhere, had to develop some system of law and order. Small fortunes in gold were carried around in little leather pouches that could easily be stolen. In fact, banks were started in the towns almost as soon as gold was discovered, but banks, too, could be robbed. The leaders of the towns appointed lawmen to take care of the robbers, horse thieves, and murderers. One of the more famous lawmen was Leadville's Martin Duggan, who reportedly rid the booming town of a gang of thieves. In some mining communities, the miners formed courts that tried the desperadoes and even hanged them from the nearest tree. This period did not last long, however, because the possibility of statehood (and respectability) was quickly on the horizon after the first gold rush.

Central City in the Colorado Territory

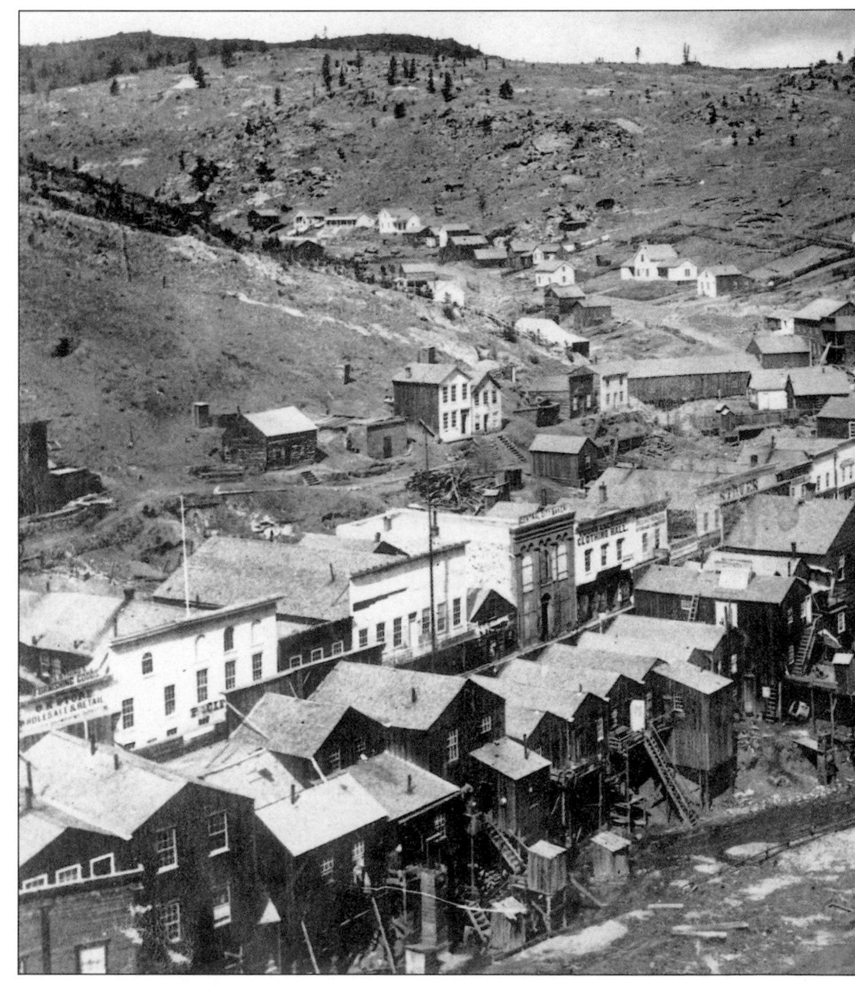

Building a New State

At the time gold was discovered in 1858, the region that would become Colorado was split up among four different American territories: Kansas, Nebraska, Utah, and New Mexico. Because the governments for those territories were a long way from the gold-fields, the miners tried to establish a new government, which they called Arapahoe County.

They tried first to attach their new county to Kansas Territory. When no action was taken by the federal government, the miners decided to create an entirely new territory, which they called Jefferson. However, they refused to vote in favor of taxing themselves, and their new government faded away.

The federal government created a new Colorado Territory in February 1861 with about the same boundaries that the future state would have. The federal government was controlled by the newly created Republican Party, and all the appointments they made in Colorado were Republican. The state remained solidly Republican for the next thirty years.

The earliest settlers hoped that with huge numbers of people coming into the territory, Colorado would quickly become a state. But the government of the United States was too busy fighting the Civil War.

The Civil War

When the Civil War started between northern and southern states in the East, Coloradans became involved, too. The 1st Colorado Cavalry was raised in 1862. The men fought well in New Mexico,

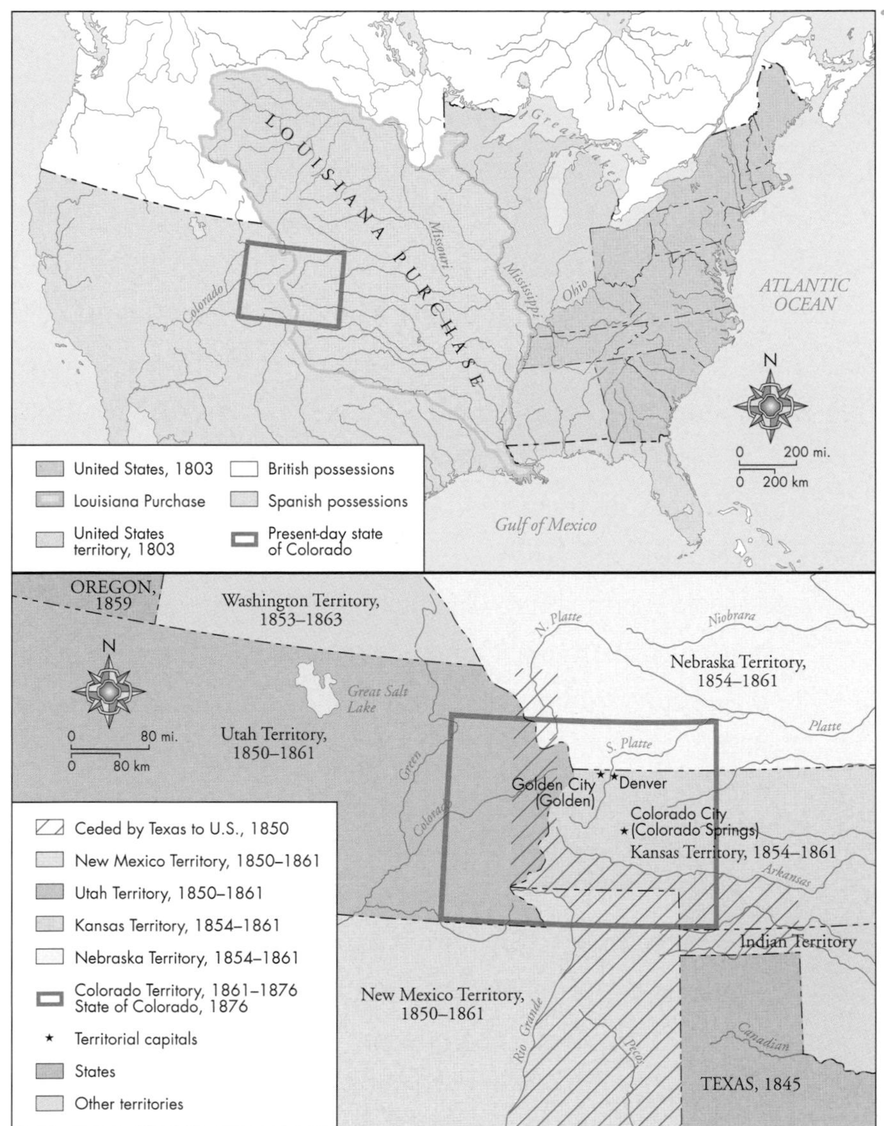

Historical map of Colorado

helping other Union troops stop the Confederate states from extending their influence all the way to California.

During the war, southern Cheyenne frequently threatened settlers. When a family was murdered by Indians, the entire Denver area panicked. Volunteers quickly formed the 3rd Colorado Cavalry. The troopers had more enthusiasm than experience.

In the autumn of 1864, Cheyenne and Arapaho chiefs surrendered to the military at Fort Lyon, hoping to bargain with the territorial governor, John Evans. The Native Americans were sent away to wait. About 700 men, women, and children, under the leadership of Black Kettle, a Cheyenne, settled about 40 miles (64 km) away from Fort Lyon, on Sand Creek.

Colonel John Chivington and his troopers of the 3rd Cavalry—probably 750 of them—took advantage of bad weather and dark nights to sneak into the Sand Creek camp on November 29, 1864. Chivington gave orders that no one was to be left alive. During a full day of fighting, many Cheyenne and Arapaho were killed.

John Evans served as Colorado territorial governor.

Afterward, rumors and exaggerated tales spread, and the numbers killed grew and grew. No one knows just how many Indians or how many soldiers died. It may have been as many as 300 Native Americans and as few as 10 soldiers; but Americans were shocked. The 3rd Cavalry became known as the "Bloody Third."

Three different government inquiries found Colonel Chivington guilty of unworthy conduct. During one inquiry, mountain man Jim Beckwourth testified that Chivington said before the fight, "I don't tell you to kill all ages and sex, but look back on the plains of the Platte where your mothers, fathers, brothers, sisters, have been slain. . . ."

"The Crow"

Jim Beckwourth (sometimes spelled "Beckwith") was a Virginia-born African-American who went to the Rocky Mountains in the 1820s as a fur trader. He established a friendship with some Crow people and lived with the tribe for some years, taking the permanent nickname of "The Crow." While meandering through the mountains of the West, he discovered a pass in the Sierra Nevadas that opened up the Sacramento Valley to settlement. It is called Beckwourth Pass.

Beckwourth was working as a shopkeeper in Denver when the Civil War started. He served as a scout for Colonel John Chivington's 3rd Colorado Cavalry. He lived in Denver until his death in 1867. He was famous for the bragging tales he told of his life in the mountains. No one knows how much he made up.

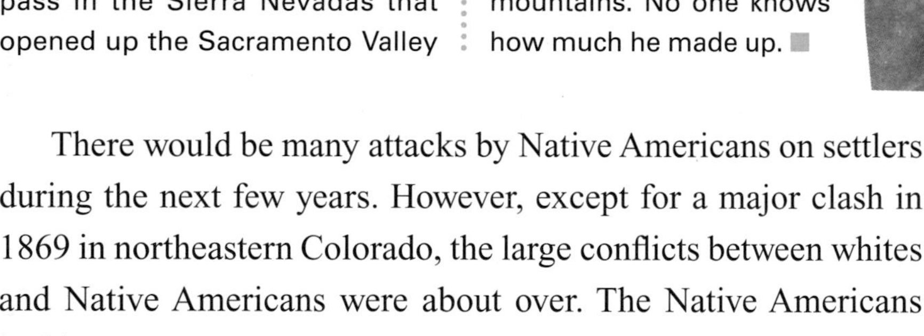

There would be many attacks by Native Americans on settlers during the next few years. However, except for a major clash in 1869 in northeastern Colorado, the large conflicts between whites and Native Americans were about over. The Native Americans had lost.

CHAPTER THREE

The Last Frontier State

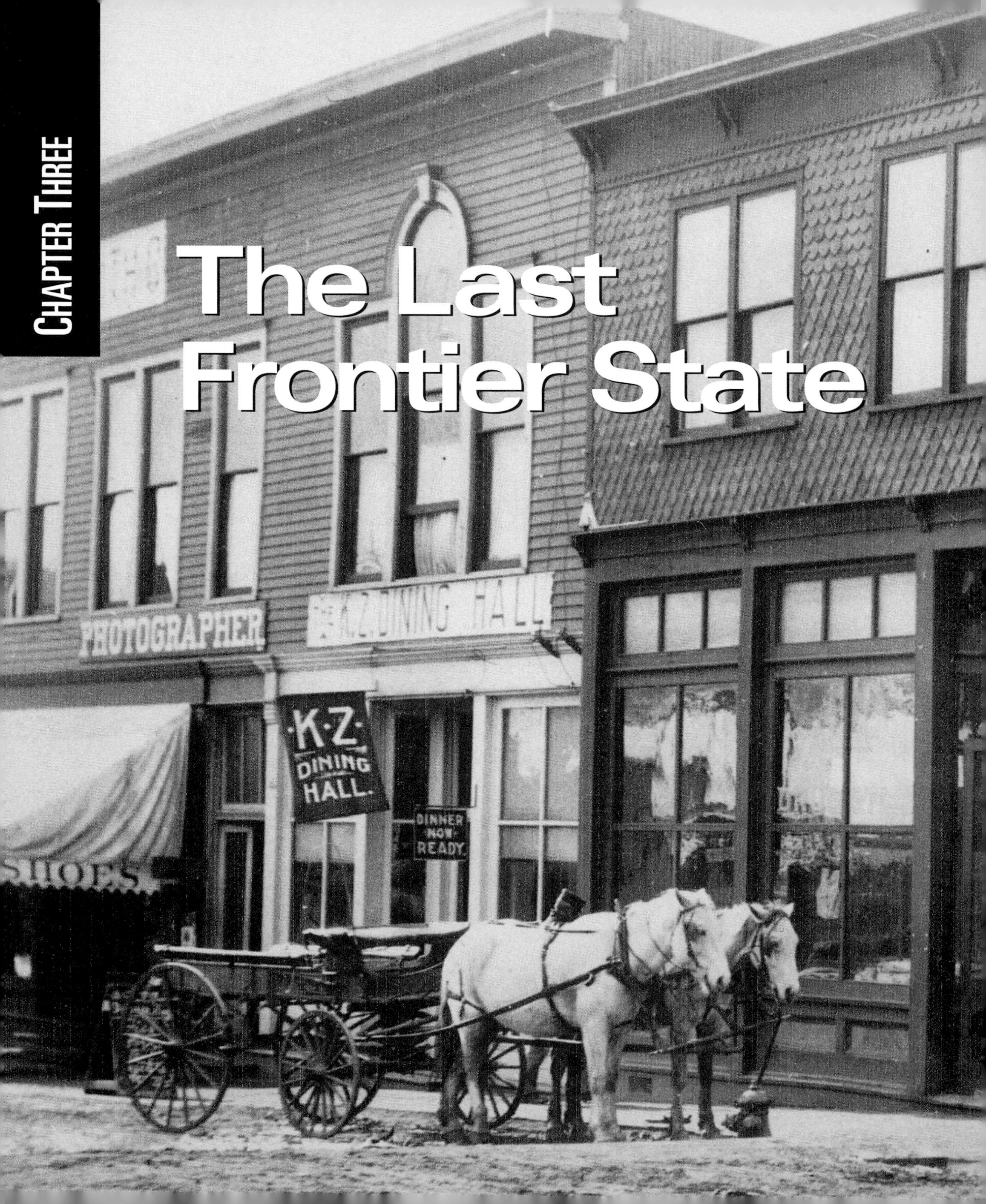

Lack of gold resulted in many Colorado ghost towns.

By the end of the Civil War, word had spread that it wasn't really easy to discover gold. The population of Colorado Territory dropped sharply as disappointed prospectors moved on. Already ghost towns lurked in the mountains as little gold turned up after the initial discoveries. Nevertheless, the easterners who had invested in Colorado thought that its beautiful setting was as important as gold. They wanted to see Colorado grow . . . and quickly.

Their answer was publicity. They wanted to get easterners and Europeans to come and see what Colorado had to offer. Cameras, which were first widely used during the Civil War, came west with the gold seekers. Colorado was one of the first states to have most of its settlement history recorded on film.

Railroads and Statehood

When the Union Pacific Railway crossed the West, it bypassed Denver, despite the best efforts of the territory's promoters. The railway developers, who had no desire to tackle the mountains, chose to run the line through Wyoming. Denver businessmen who were sure Colorado had a future started the Denver Pacific Railway

Opposite: Cripple Creek in 1895

William Jackson Palmer built the Denver & Rio Grande Railroad.

to connect Denver and Cheyenne, Wyoming, in 1870. The city was also connected to Kansas City by the Kansas Pacific.

One believer in Colorado's future was William Jackson Palmer, an old railroad man. He built the Denver & Rio Grande Railroad, a north-south line that opened up the mountains. He had the foresight to build the line where he hoped development would happen rather than where it already had. Pueblo, Trinidad, and Colorado Springs were among the cities that developed because of the railroad. As these towns attracted settlers, Colorado quickly acquired the 40,000 residents required for a territory to become a state.

Colorado was admitted to the union on August 1, 1876, just after the hundredth anniversary of the Declaration of Independence. For that reason, the state has always been called the Centennial State.

Ouray and the Utes

Nathan Meeker was an Ohio-born journalist who worked during the 1870s to help create a cooperative agricultural community called Union Colony in the new town of Greeley. Individuals owned their own land, but anything implemented to help all of them, such as irrigation systems, was owned by all. In 1878, Meeker became an Indian agent, working with the Utes on the White River.

Meeker thought that the Utes would be better off if they adopted "American" ways of thinking and acting. Unfortunately, this was at the same time that the governor of Colorado seized most of the Utes' mountain land and opened it to settlement by whites. Thus, the Utes were pushed into the far western and southern section of the state, and even that area was wanted by businessmen.

In truth, the whites wanted any excuse to take away more land,

The destruction following the Ute attack against Nathaniel Meeker

and the Utes gave it to them. Meeker, upset that the Native Americans weren't paying any attention to his ideas, called for troopers to help him. Feeling threatened by the show of force, the Utes attacked, killing Meeker and eleven others.

White developers were already laying their plans for the newly opened land when Chief Ouray and other leaders agreed to give up their western lands in return for reservations in Utah. Within weeks, Grand Junction—still the major town in western Colorado—was being built. Prospectors located mineral ores, and new mining towns, especially Durango, grew almost overnight.

Several small Ute groups managed to hang on to small segments of land in the southwestern corner of the state. Today, these are the Ute Mountain and Southern Ute reservations.

Leadville in the 1870s

Another Boom

When the gold boom went bust at Oro City in California Gulch, a foresighted prospector had assayed some of the strange red material that most miners tossed aside. It turned out to be lead ore with sustantial amounts of silver. This brought a new boom—a silver one; it also brought a new name to the growing town—Leadville.

Leadville quickly sprawled up the mountainside. Eastern writers called it "Cloud City," and illustrious people looking for a reason to travel paid it a visit as soon as the railroad reached it in 1880. Former president Ulysses Grant rode that first train in. Famed figure of the Wild West Doc Holliday worked at a Leadville gambling hall for a while. British playwright Oscar Wilde gave a lecture to an enthusiastic audience there.

The miners who worked the mines around Leadville worked hard all day under dangerous conditions. At night, they played. Leadville and every town like it had more saloons and gambling halls than any other kinds of business.

In 1891, a cowhand who would rather have been a prospector found gold at Cripple Creek, a stream that was notorious for tripping up cattle. His find signaled the beginning of a series of gold finds that turned the Cripple Creek area into the largest producer of gold in the United States for several years. In an area only 6 miles square (15.5 sq km), miners sank more than 5,000 shafts into the earth.

During the next twenty years, between $15 million and $20 million a year was brought out of those mountains. The mines turned nearby Colorado Springs into a burgeoning and wealthy community.

Many of the silver towns, however, were destined to turn into ghost towns. For twenty years, the U.S. government had supported the price of silver, keeping it artificially high to maintain a healthy mining industry. Simply, it paid high prices for the metal even when it knew it could not sell it for so much. In 1893, though, it stopped that price support, and the bottom dropped out of the Colorado silver-mining industry. Gradually, people began to move away, and many beautiful little towns began to deteriorate.

Governor James Peabody used the state's National Guard to fight strikers.

The Strikers and the Owners

Like industries elsewhere, the mining companies of Colorado during the early part of the twentieth century faced many strikes by their workers. The owners were used to having total control, but the workers were beginning to feel they had rights that weren't recognized. They wanted to form organizations called unions to help them.

For the most part, the Colorado government backed the business owners and let them do whatever they wanted to stop workers going on strike—even if what they did was illegal. Governor James Peabody used the National Guard (a state's reserve military organization) to fight the strikers. People died on both sides, and both sides

One of the strikes that preceded the Ludlow Massacre

committed terrible acts that angered Colorado citizens.

The worst time came in 1913, when coal miners in the southern part of the state went on strike against the dangerous conditions in the coal mines. In April 1914, guardsmen fired into a tent colony at Ludlow, killing women and children as well as some strikers. The nation was shocked at the "Ludlow Massacre," and President Woodrow Wilson sent in federal troops to quiet both sides.

The distant owner of the coal mines was billionaire John D. Rockefeller Jr. He appeared to give in to the workers' demand for a union by forming a "company union," but the organization had no power. Strikes, often violent, continued to disturb Colorado's peace for years to come.

Hoping to show the rest of the nation that the Ludlow Massacre was not typical of Colorado, the people of the state became avid supporters of the United States's entry into World War I. The people who ran the cattle feedlots in the eastern part of the state, and the miners in the mountains, all agreed to work even harder to provide U.S. soldiers with what they needed to fight in Europe.

A Period of Fear

Immediately following World War I, many Americans tried to blame the newly arrived economic depression on communists, who were establishing the new Soviet Union. Out of the fear of communists, fear of all foreigners began to spread. The Colorado legislature made it illegal to criticize Colorado. Soon this fear of foreigners turned into a fear of any people different from oneself.

Colorado suffered, as much of the nation did, from the activities of the Ku Klux Klan.

An organization called the Ku Klux Klan (KKK) had been formed after the Civil War. All over the country, millions of white Protestants formed a "brotherhood" to take action against everyone else: blacks, immigrants, Roman Catholics, Jews. The action usually began with harassment of others. Sometimes, Klan members boycotted businesses owned by people the "Invisible Empire" did not like. Not infrequently, the harassment would become violent, with the lynching (illegal hanging) of the minorities. Colorado's Hispanic people began to live in fear.

In 1923, a Denver Klan member, Benjamin F. Stapleton, was elected mayor of the city. He named many other Klan members to important posts, even to judgeships. He was reelected with a huge majority, giving power to the KKK. The following year, the Klan was powerful enough to elect Klan members as the governor of the state and the new member of the U.S. Senate. At least one member of the state supreme court was a member of the Klan.

Fortunately, there were enough non-Klan members in the General Assembly of Colorado to prevent harsh measures against immigrants and Catholics from being turned into law. Mayor Stapleton himself turned against the state's Klan leader, the Grand

Dragon. The general public, which had not paid much attention to what was going on, began to oppose the Klan. Gradually, the power of the Invisible Empire dwindled. Stapleton himself kept being elected to the position of Denver mayor until 1947. When Denver's first big airport was built, it was named for him.

The Great Depression brought unemployment and hunger to Colorado.

The Great Depression

Colorado agriculture and mining had boomed during World War I, but prices and the need for metals plummeted after the war. Even the new molybdenum mines—a metallic element essential in strengthening steel—had to shut down. Coal, which had been a big seller throughout the nation, was being replaced by petroleum. The state went into an economic depression.

Conditions got worse when the New York stock markets collapsed in 1929. Most Coloradans were certain they wouldn't be affected. The spreading depression took a couple of years to reach them, but in 1931, the crash had destroyed the market for the metals mined in Colorado's mountains.

When word spread that Colorado was in economic trouble, people stopped moving to the mountain state. Colorado's growth rate slowed to only a third of what it had been during earlier decades.

During the Great Depression, many Coloradans were given work through federal work programs. The people working for the Civilian Conservation Corps (CCC) did a great deal for Colorado on federal lands. Parks were improved, roads were built, trees were planted. Even the mountain streams were stocked with baby trout. Laborers for the Works Progress Administration (WPA)—renamed Works Projects Administration in 1939—built schools, recreation centers, dams on rivers, city halls, and even tennis courts and hospitals. One project constructed the Colorado–Big Thompson tunnel, which fed western water into the eastern farmlands.

Workers in the Civilian Conservation Corps

The Hispanic citizens of Colorado were not so successful at finding work as the whites during the Depression. Officials decided that any man with a Hispanic name should become a farm laborer, even if the work didn't pay enough to support his family.

As the decade of depression was drawing to a close, the United States crept toward involvement in another major war in Europe. Conditions at home began to improve as factories were put to work making materials for war.

Chapter Four

A New Frontier of Technology

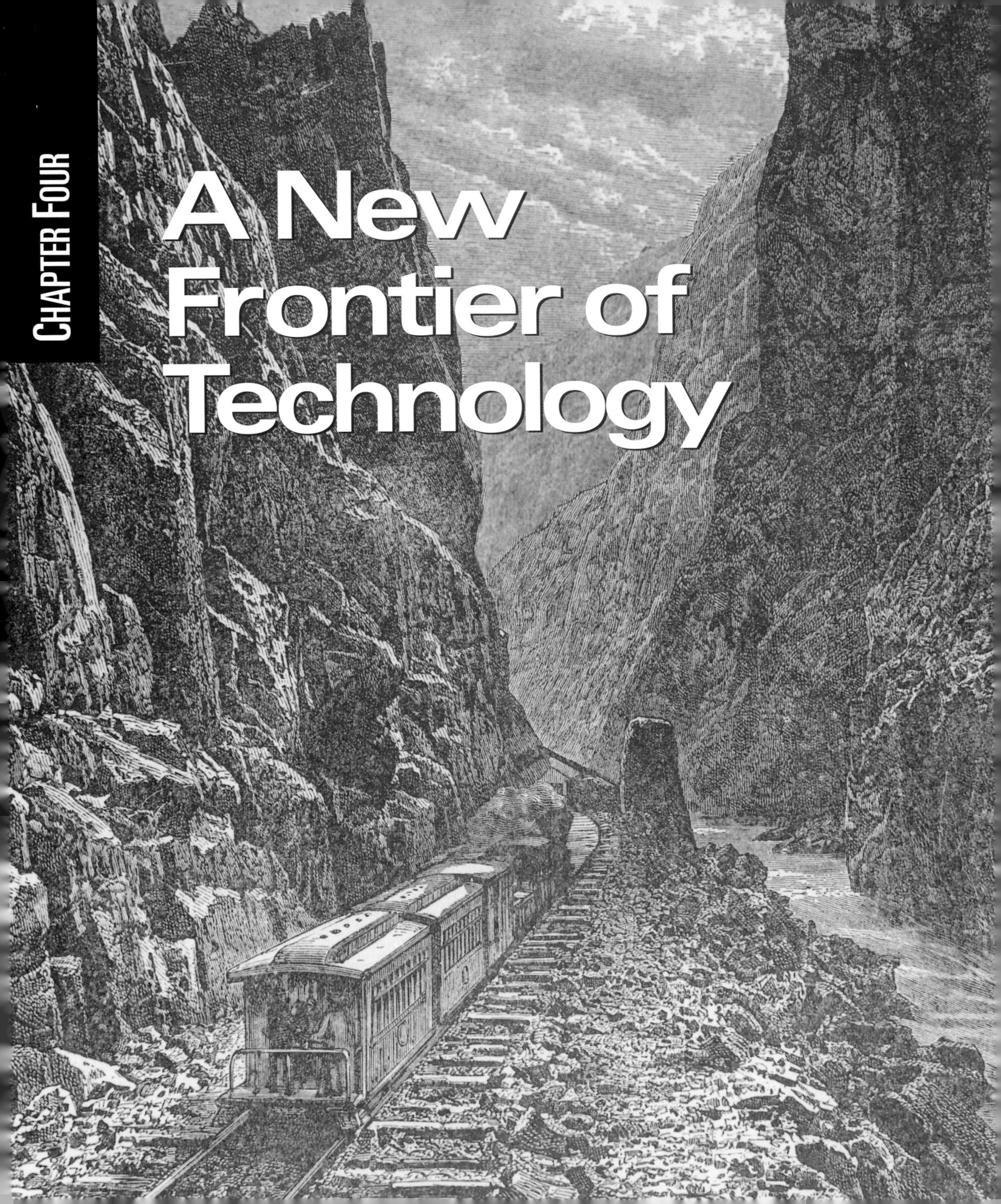

Japanese civilians being sent to a camp near Granada during World War II

The 1940s and the beginning of what became World War II brought a new boom to Colorado. Denver donated land for a major U.S. Army Air Corps base. That base and the new Rocky Mountain Arsenal brought thousands of people and plenty of jobs to the area.

Leadville was chosen as a base for training troops in mountain and snow skills. The molybdenum mine at Climax, which had just been coasting along, suddenly revved up for full production. The metal would be needed in military aircraft. Even agriculture started to boom as a greatly increased military needed to be fed.

The biggest new wartime plant in Colorado was the Denver Ordnance Plant, which made ammunition. Thousands of women worked there throughout the war. After the war was won, the huge complex of buildings was turned into a major federal office center. The federal government is still one of the biggest employers in Colorado.

Colorado, National Defense, and Technology

Uranium was discovered in southwestern Colorado. This became a very important resource in the years following World War II because uranium was used in making atomic bombs and is still

Opposite: Colorado's Royal Gorge

Outside and Inside the Fences

The Japanese bombed Pearl Harbor in Hawaii on December 7, 1941, and the United States entered the war in both Asia and Europe. President Franklin D. Roosevelt signed an order requiring that all people of Japanese ancestry in the states along the Pacific Coast be moved away from the area—in case they were spies. Some of these Japanese people were sent to a camp near Granada, Colorado, where they lived for more than three years behind barbed wire.

At the same time, the Japanese American people who lived in Denver were allowed to carry on with their normal lives. The governor, Ralph Carr, refused to assume that all Japanese Americans were dangerous. When the war ended, many of the detained Japanese Americans stayed in Colorado, rather than return to the West Coast. ■

used in nuclear power plants. Uranium processing was carried out in several towns around Durango.

In 1958, the U.S. Air Force opened its new university at Colorado Springs. It was the air force's answer to the army's West Point and the navy's Annapolis. At the same time, work was begun on tearing out the center of Cheyenne Mountain near Colorado Springs. Built into the inside of the mountain—mounted on huge springs so that it could not move if the area were bombed—is the North American Aerospace Defense Command, called NORAD. The bomb-proof headquarters was built during the cold war, when the United States thought that the Soviet Union might send missiles to knock out important U.S. facilities.

Inside the North American Aerospace Defense Command near Colorado Springs

After the war, Colorado did not fall back

into its old pattern of concentrating on agriculture and mining. Instead, businesses moved there to take advantage of all the people who had discovered the outdoor life. Martin Marietta Aerospace Corporation began to build missiles in the Denver area, and many other industries requiring technically trained people also moved in.

After the Soviet Union collapsed and its many republics became separate countries in 1991, most of Colorado's technological work came to involve computers and communications instead of weapons.

Missiles are among the products of the Martin Marietta Aerospace Corporation

The Used-Up Rivers

Colorado's technological skills will need to be applied to a very different area in coming years: water. In the 1880s, large boats were able to ascend the Colorado River. They carried supplies to the mining camps and growing towns. To make the trip, boats had to start at the river's mouth, where torrents of water tumbled into the Gulf of California. It took brave navigators to churn through the rough waters of the Colorado River.

Today, barely a drop of water reaches the Gulf of California from the Colorado River. Where does the water that carved out the Grand Canyon go? It is literally used up along the way. The Colorado River has been called the "lifeblood of the Southwest." It feeds the big cities of Las Vegas, Nevada; Los Angeles and San Diego, California; and Phoenix, Arizona.

All the states and the nation of Mexico along the river need their share of the river's water. But what is "their share"? The seven states through which the river moves wrote the Colorado River Compact in 1922. It allotted each of the states the right to take a certain amount of water out of the river. In 1944, a similar treaty also gave Mexico the right to Colorado River water. Unfortunately, the calculations used to figure how much each state could take were made on bad information. In addition, the compact did not take into account the tremendous population and business growth of California, Arizona, and Nevada. Consequently, the water of the Colorado River does not even last long enough to reach the river's mouth in the Gulf of California. Today, all the water is used up. River water and how to move it is going to be a central issue in Colorado in coming years because the underground water of the high plains is also being used up.

The Colorado River has been called the "lifeblood of the Southwest."

Groundwater often exists in huge underground rivers called aquifers. When people drill wells, they are drilling into an aquifer. A mammoth aquifer called the Ogallala exists under the Great Plains states from Texas up into South Dakota. In 1990, water experts estimated that about 4 percent, or 131 million acre-feet, of the aquifer was located beneath eastern Colorado. Found at the beginning of the century, the Ogallala was not used much until the 1950s. Today, the aquifer provides much of the water used for irrigation of crops, as well as drinking water in some places.

Shifting the Water

The major factor affecting life in Colorado is that most of the usable agricultural land is on the eastern side of the Rockies, while the water supplies are on the western side. In the last fifty years, humans have done much to try to change that situation.

One project is called the Colorado–Big Thompson. Run by the federal government, it takes water from Shadow Mountain Lake on the Colorado River around Rocky Mountain National Park and sends it through a 13-mile (21-km) tunnel in the mountains to the Big Thompson River on the eastern side of the Continental Divide. The Moffat Tunnel, built in the 1920s, carries both water and railway trains through the mountains.

More than thirty years ago, another water project was discussed. Called the Animas–LaPlata Project, the project was designed to take water from the Animas River near Durango and pump it uphill. This project would have required the construction of two dams and 200 miles (322 km) of canals. The Animas– LaPlata Project didn't get off the ground at that time, but in recent years, it has been discussed

again. Critics of the plan point out that it will cost much more to water an acre of farmland than that acre could ever earn in crops.

All Coloradans must be involved in decisions about water use. There are several important arguments against starting new projects to shift water from one side of the state to the other. Some have to do with the environment—ecologists and others fear that more rivers could run dry the way the Colorado River has. Another problem is that if the people in the eastern cities keep getting plenty of water, those cities will continue growing and demanding more water. It will be an endless cycle.

Colorado's future depends on water. New answers must be sought.

Colorado can be dry and relies on a dependable water supply.

Tolerance for Some

Colorado was among the first states to establish open-housing laws, meaning that housing for rent or purchase had to be available to anyone, regardless of race. But that tolerance has not extended in recent years to homosexuals (people who are attracted to other people of the same sex).

In the 1980s, local governments, especially in resort communities, sometimes passed laws that protected homosexuals from discrimination. Many Coloradans thought homosexuality was wrong and should not be given such protection. In 1992, a majority of voters approved a new state law that would prevent such local laws from being passed. Immediately, people who opposed such discrimination against homosexuals (led by the cities of Aspen and Vail) took the new law to court. Also, many national businesses and organizations that had intended to hold conventions in Colorado canceled their meetings, harming the tourist industry. In 1996, the U.S. Supreme Court said that Colorado's law violated the U.S. Constitution and must not be enforced.

Intolerance for Juvenile Crime

One thing that Coloradans are no longer tolerating is juvenile crime. Because gang warfare and juvenile crime were increasing rapidly, many teenagers are now being treated as adults and sent to prison. The state founded the Youth Offender System (YOS) in 1994 to send convicted teenagers between the ages of 14 and 18 to army-style boot camp. Instead of just lingering in prison, they do a lot of physical training, schooling, and psychological evaluation. The YOS facility is in Pueblo.

Tourism, technology, tolerance—and above all, water—will continue to be important issues for Colorado in coming years.

Chapter Five

Shining Peaks and Fertile Plains

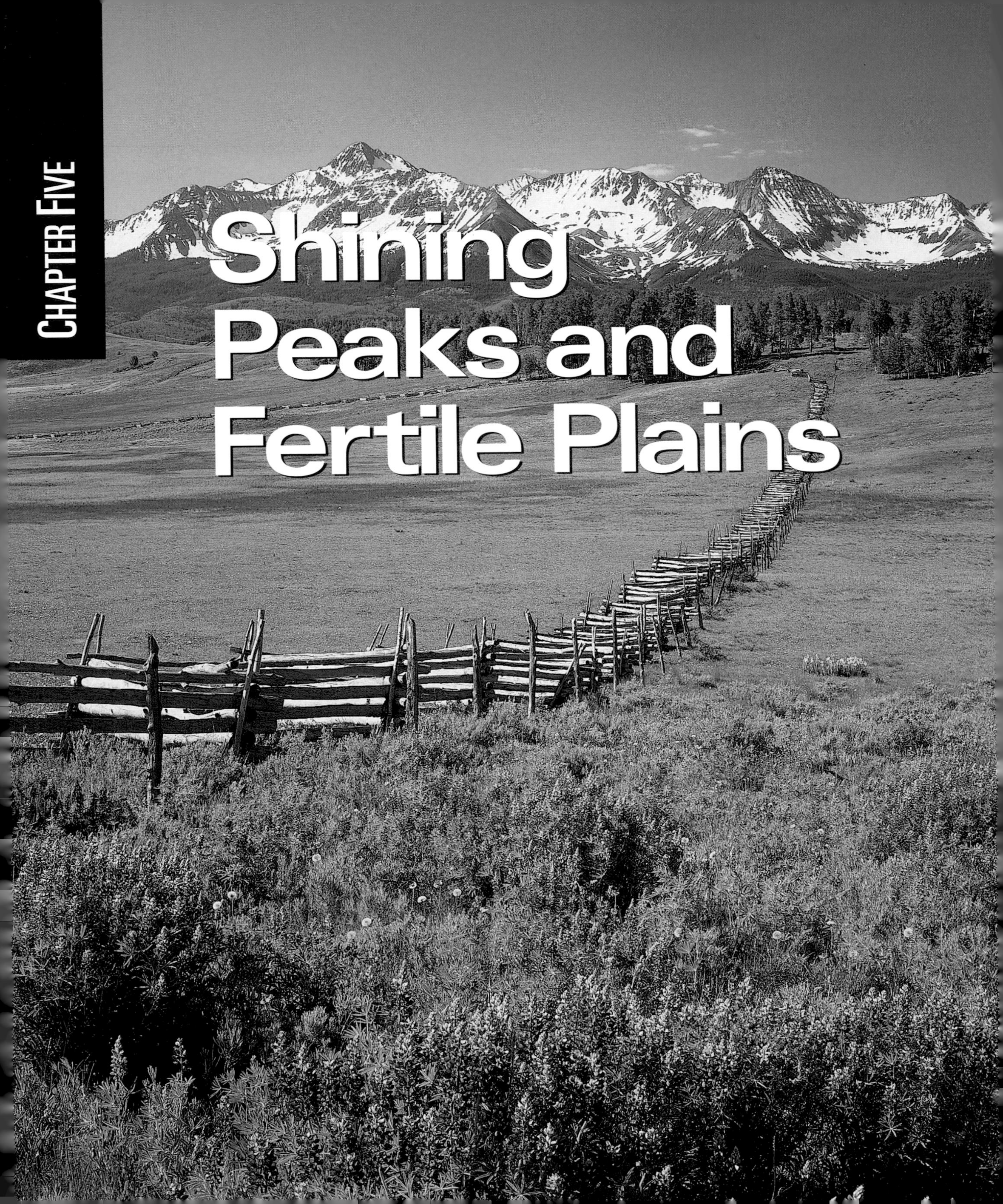

The Rocky Mountains are a vital part of Colorado's landscape.

The Native Americans called the Rocky Mountains the "Shining Mountains." Even today, the name *Colorado* brings mountains to mind. Yet even the simplest map shows that mountains occupy only one-third of the state, running from north to south. The eastern two-fifths of the state is an extension of the Great Plains of Kansas and Nebraska. West of the mountains is another mostly flat region called the Colorado Plateau. Nevertheless, it's the splendid mountains that draw most people to Colorado.

The Southern Rockies

About the time dinosaurs disappeared, a new episode of mountain building began on Earth. Many geologists believe that the continents are carried on huge chunks of the Earth's crust that float on the molten interior of the planet. These huge chunks, called plates, take thousands of years to move only a few inches. Occasionally, however, that motion is enough to make the plates run into each other. The collision of the plates makes the land where the two plates meet thrust upward into mountains.

Opposite: Wilson's Peak near Telluride

The upthrusting of plates that created the Rocky Mountains began about 70 million years ago. The Rocky Mountains run from Canada southward through Mexico. The mountains in Colorado are called the Southern Rockies. The Southern Rockies make up a distinct section of the Rocky Mountain system because a flat plainlike area called the Wyoming Basin creates a large gap in the range. It's this gap that trains run through to avoid having to climb mountains.

Within Colorado, two belts of ranges divide the state. The eastern belt includes the Front Range, the Wet Mountains, and the Sangre de Cristo ("Blood of Christ") Mountains. The western belt is made up of the San Juans, the Sawatch Mountains, and the Park Range. In addition, a section of Wyoming's Medicine Bow Range extends toward Cameron Pass in the Front Range.

The Continental Divide

Pikes Peak is so famous that many people mistakenly think it's the highest mountain in Colorado. It isn't. Pikes Peak is "only" 14,110 feet (4,301 m) high, but it is fairly isolated, so it stands out on the horizon. Reaching it became a dream for prospectors and settlers, who could see it from far away. They often put signs on their wagons that read PIKES PEAK OR BUST!

More than 1,140 mountains in Colorado reach above 10,000 feet (3,048 m). Fifty-four of those are Fourteeners, mountains that are more than 14,000 feet (4,267 m) high. If you could draw a line from the top of one high peak to the top of the next through the Rocky Mountains, you would be drawing in North America's Continental Divide. The divide is an imaginary line generally marking

Never Summer Range

the change from rivers that flow eastward into the Atlantic Ocean to those that flow westward, eventually reaching the Pacific Ocean.

The Continental Divide meanders back and forth between the Front Range, the Medicine Bows, and the Sawatch Mountains. The highest point within the Sawatch Mountains, and the highest point in Colorado, is Mount Elbert at 14,433 feet (4,399 m). It is the second-highest peak in the contiguous forty-eight states.

Three less mountainous—and treeless!—bowls between the ranges are called North Park, Middle Park, and South Park. Between North and Middle Park is a rocky region called the Rabbit Ears Range. A similar park (and the largest of them) is the San Luis Valley in the south-central part of the state.

The Eastern Plains

From the vantage point of the middle of eastern Colorado, it's quite unlikely to even see a hill, let alone the mountains for which the state is famous. Those mountains lie farther west. Eastern Colorado is part of the Great Plains, geologically more similar to Kansas than to the mountains.

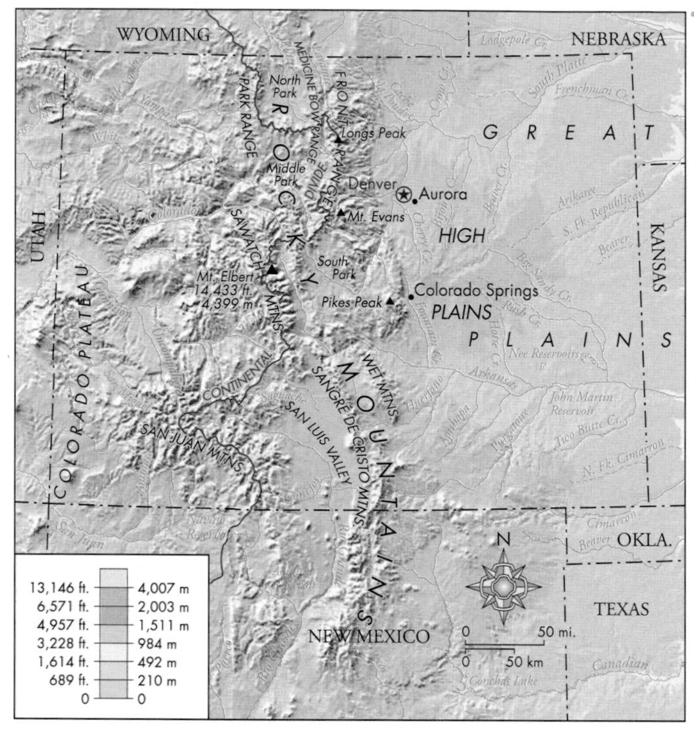

Colorado's topography

The land of the plains does rise toward the center of the continent, though, giving them the name High Plains. Colorado's plains are divided into the High Plains and the Piedmont. The Piedmont is the area along the valleys of the two major rivers in eastern Colorado, the South Platte and the Arkansas. The rest of the terrain in that part of the state belongs to the High Plains. They are referred to as "High" Plains, because, although the open flat countryside is the Great Plains, the country is actually rising to a higher and higher elevation as one nears the mountains.

Colorado's lowest point is along the Arkansas River in Prowers County, where the river crosses into Kansas. But this lowest point is higher than many states' highest point, 3,350 feet (1,021 m) above sea level.

Early surveyors for the U.S. government came into Colorado along the major High Plains rivers—and they didn't like what they saw. In 1820, Major Stephen Long traveled down the South Platte River. He had already traveled through hundreds of miles of plains, and Colorado looked like just more of the same. A botanist in Long's group found such plains "fatiguing to the spirit." Long was particularly dismayed by the sight of mile after mile of sand dunes along the South Platte. The written report from Major Long's expedition described northeastern Colorado as "uninhabitable"

Grasses along the High Plains

and "wholly unfit for cultivation." Travelers from the East, seeking places to settle, believed Long's report and bypassed Colorado's "Great American Desert" on their way to California.

The Colorado Plateau

The western side of the Rockies is called the Western Slope. Most of it consists of the Colorado Plateau. This is a predominantly flat but elevated area occupying 130,000 square miles (336,700 sq km) in the Four Corners region where Colorado, New Mexico, Arizona, and Utah meet. When the land was rising, creating the mountains, only the flat land of the Colorado Plateau resisted the upthrusting. It rose, too, but all as one solid mass, not as individual peaks.

The Colorado River, which rises in Middle Park, and its tributaries have moved across the plateau for millions of years, gradually digging away at the stone under the rivers as the plateau was raised up. It was the rising of the plateau that created one of Earth's great spectaculars—the Grand Canyon of the Colorado River in Arizona. Colorado, too, has its canyons.

A peach orchard on the Colorado Plateau

Southwestern Colorado is called tableland. Its mountains have flat tops called mesas. These mesas used to be fertile and green, which is why that part of the state is called Mesa Verde, meaning "green mesa." Starting around 500 B.C., Native Americans occupied the great tablelands of southwestern Colorado, northeastern Arizona, and northern New Mexico. The countryside is no longer green, however.

The Rivers

Some say Colorado's rivers define its sections. The two great rivers of eastern Colorado tie the state to the plains: the Colorado River links Colorado to the mountainous West, and the Rio Grande, which rises in the San Juan Mountains, makes southern Colorado part of the Great Southwest.

Though the Colorado River starts as a mere trickle, it is soon joined by a number of tributaries. These tributaries include the Little Colorado, Gunnison, Dolores, San Juan, Green, White, and Gila Rivers. Before 1921, the section of the Colorado River

The Dolores River Canyon

upstream from where the Green River joins it was called the Grand River, but Colorado already had a Rio Grande (meaning "Grand River"). So Coloradans persuaded the U.S. Congress to change the Grand to the Colorado. That section is now usually referred to as the Upper Colorado.

The Colorado River drains an expanse 246,000 square miles (637,140 sq km) in area. In addition to Colorado itself, this drainage area includes Utah, Wyoming, New Mexico, Nevada, Arizona, California, and a large section of Mexico. The river was first called Rio Colorado, meaning "red-colored river," by Father Francisco Thomas Garces, a missionary from Arizona in 1776. The water is red because it travels through the red-colored sandstone of the Colorado Plateau.

The Colorado River has sliced a number of spectacular canyons through the hard, colorful rock of the Colorado Plateau. Other rivers do the same. The Gunnison River, for example, has formed the little known but quite spectacular Black Canyon. The canyon is more than 50 miles (80 km) long but only 1,300 feet (396 m) wide at its narrowest point. Its dark rock gives it the name. The canyon was declared a national monument in 1933. There are three dams in the gorge of the Black Canyon. They make artificial lakes that are part of the Curecanti National Recreation Area.

A tributary of the Gunnison River is the Uncompahgre. The name derives from a Ute word meaning "red river canyon." Also rising on the western slope of the San Juans is the San Juan River of southwestern Colorado. It flows southwest through the Southern Ute Indian Reservation.

Colorado's Geographical Features

Total area; rank	104,100 sq. mi. (269,618 sq km), 8th
Land area; rank	103,729 sq. mi. (268,657sq km), 8th
Water area; rank	371 sq. mi. (960 sq km), 43rd
***Inland water;* rank**	371 sq. mi. (960 sq km), 38th
Geographic center	Park, 30 miles (48 km) northwest of Pikes Peak
Highest point	Mount Elbert, 14,433 feet (4,399 m)
Lowest point	Along the Arkansas River in Prowers County, 3,350 feet (1,021 m)
Largest city	Denver
Longest river	Colorado
Population; rank	4,301,261 (2000 census); 24th
Record high temperature	118°F (48°C) at Bennett on July 11, 1888
Record low temperature	–61°F (–52°C) at Maybell in Moffat County on February 1, 1985
Average July temperature	74°F (23°C)
Average January temperature	28°F (–2°C)
Average annual precipitation	15 inches (38 cm)

Climate

Opposite: Black Canyon was formed by the Gunnison River.

Water would not be such an issue if Colorado were not basically a dry state, despite the seemingly endless snows of winter. Cacti, which are plants of desert regions, are found throughout the state. Unlike the climate of the Great Plains to the east, Colorado has fairly warm days and quite cold nights. The vegetation must be able to withstand the regular temperature changes that occur throughout the state, so it tends to be low-growing and tough.

Denver's climate resembles that of most places in the central Great Plains. At the higher altitudes in the mountains, conditions can be quite different. For example, the average summer temperature in Denver is 73°F (23°C), but in Leadville, which is located at almost twice the elevation, the average if only 56°F (13°C). In winter, those two places average 32°F (0°C) and 25°F (–4°C) respectively.

Considerably more rain occurs in Leadville than in Denver. Denver receives only about 14 inches (35.5 cm) of precipitation

"Too Thick to Drink"

Water that trickles off the glaciers lying atop the mountains called the Never Summers in north-central Colorado forms the small beginning of the Colorado River. Before the Colorado River reaches the end of its 1,450-mile (2,334-km) journey to the Gulf of California, it provides the water that allowed the great Southwest to develop.

During that journey, the river drops almost 3 miles (5 km) in elevation and goes through forty-nine dams. It also changes color—from the red of sandstone mud that gave it its name to the greenish water that has been through so many dams that all the silt is gone. Explorer John Wesley Powell (right), who studied the Grand Canyon, described the tricky river as "too thick to drink, too thin to plow." ■

Denver can expect many winter snowstorms.

each year. Most of that falls as rain in the spring. However, the city can receive major snowstorms during most of the year except the summer months. The snow usually does not last long when it does fall. The city area receives enough moisture to keep it green, but the nearby plains turn brown early in the summer.

The mountains cause interesting things to happen in eastern Colorado. The eastern slopes of the Rocky Mountains tend to turn moving air masses into cyclones, or spinning masses of air that, in winter, carry great quantities of snow toward the Midwest. Also from the mountains come some of the most devastating hailstorms known in the United States. The small hard pebbles of ice fall almost without warning, usually in the spring when winter wheat crops are just about ready for harvesting. The High Plains are sometimes affected by unexpected warm winds called chinooks descending from the mountains as well.

Dinosaur Country

Colorado was not always dry. Long before the mountains started to form, the land was a swamp that supported dinosaurs. Colorado had only just become a state when paleontologists (scientists who study fossil life) began to find the huge bones of these ancient reptiles.

The largest finds were made in 1909, when Earl Douglass, an eager fossil hunter from the Carnegie Museum in Pittsburgh, Pennsylvania, located Brontosaurus (now called Apatosaurus) bones. Over the following years, at least a dozen new species of dinosaurs were found in the area. Eventually, so many remains were found in a single dry rock quarry of the Uinta Mountains of northwestern Colorado and adjacent Utah that the beautiful canyon area in which they were found was preserved as Dinosaur National Monument.

Tracks left in ancient mud (now turned to rock) by a Tyrannosaurus rex are visible near Bent's Fort on the shore of the Purgatoire River. Triceratops prints are found nearby.

Today's Wildlife

Colorado may be a mountain state, but the state bird is a prairie bird, the lark bunting. The state flower, the Rocky Mountain columbine, and the state animal, the bighorn sheep, nevertheless, are both inhabitants of the mountains.

Mountain lions, elk, mule deer, and black bears are fairly common at a distance from the cities. The grizzly bear was long thought to be extinct in Colorado. Then in 1979, a single bear was found and shot in the San Juan Mountains.

On a smaller scale, two widely known insect pests reflect the state by their names. The Colorado potato beetle is a pest of potato, eggplant, and tomato crops; Colorado tick fever is a flu-like virus carried by the wood tick.

The bighorn sheep, Colorado's state animal, lives among the mountains.

The unusual axolotl is a resident of Colorado (and only Mexico City besides). It is a salamander that, unlike other salamanders, does not change as it grows into adulthood. Salamanders normally lose their gills and turn very lizardlike. Axolotls are also known as tiger salamanders.

Plant Life

The vegetation in Colorado changes with elevation the way it changes with long north-south distances in the open plains. The center of San Luis Valley, for example, has vegetation similar to that of the open grazing plains of Texas. Yet, only a few miles away, the tops of the mountains are barren of trees.

Below the tree line, most mountains are covered with coniferous forest. The conifers may differ, depending on which side of the mountains they grow. On the north side, most trees are Douglas fir. On the south side, they are likely to be ponderosa pines. An important low-growing conifer is the Colorado piñon. It has an edible seed, the pine nut, or pignolia.

Aspens are poplar trees with leaves that have flattened stems causing them to shiver in even the slightest breeze. These are called quaking aspens. They are most noticeable in the autumn

Colorado's parks and forests

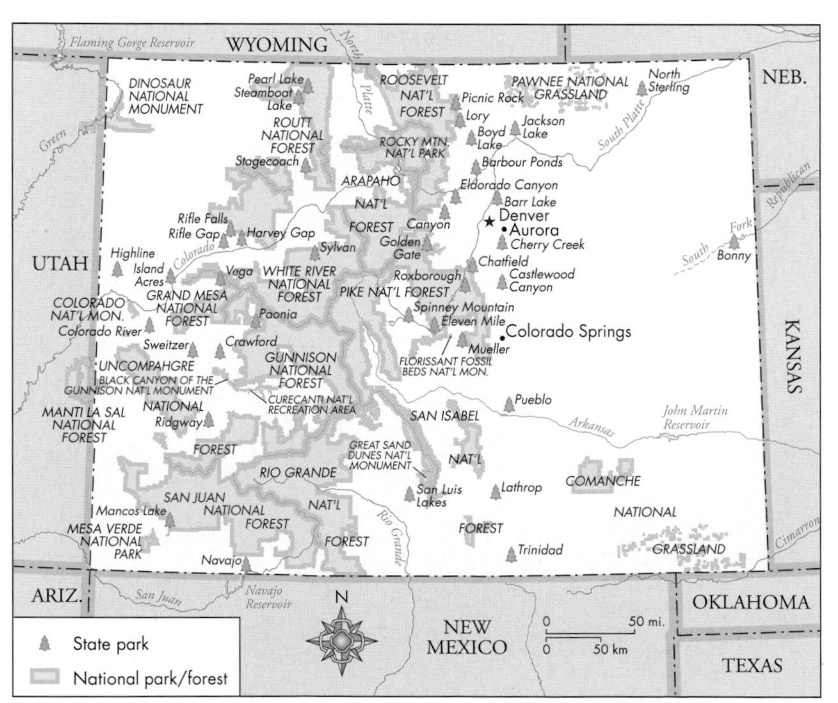

A moonrise over the White River National Forest

after the shimmering green trees have turned golden, lighting up the mountainsides.

The first national forest was created in Colorado in 1891 by President Benjamin Harrison. That initial preserve became Colorado's White River National Forest. The forest lies around the bowl in which the skiing community of Vail lies. Today, there are twelve national forests either wholly or partly in Colorado.

On the plains are two regions called national grasslands. These are an outgrowth of the long drought in the late 1920s and early 1930s that affected the region covering some of Oklahoma, Texas, southeastern Colorado, southwestern Kansas, and northwestern New Mexico. The land became so dry that the slightest breeze stirred up the soil and carried it away. The region was called the Dust Bowl. During the following years, Colorado's Dust Bowl was planted by the federal government with grass that had roots that would hold the soil to the ground. Farmers were paid not to return to planting grain, which would expose the soil again. The Pawnee National Grassland is in the north, and the Comanche National Grassland is in the south.

Chapter Six

Cities, Mountains, and Cliff Dwellings

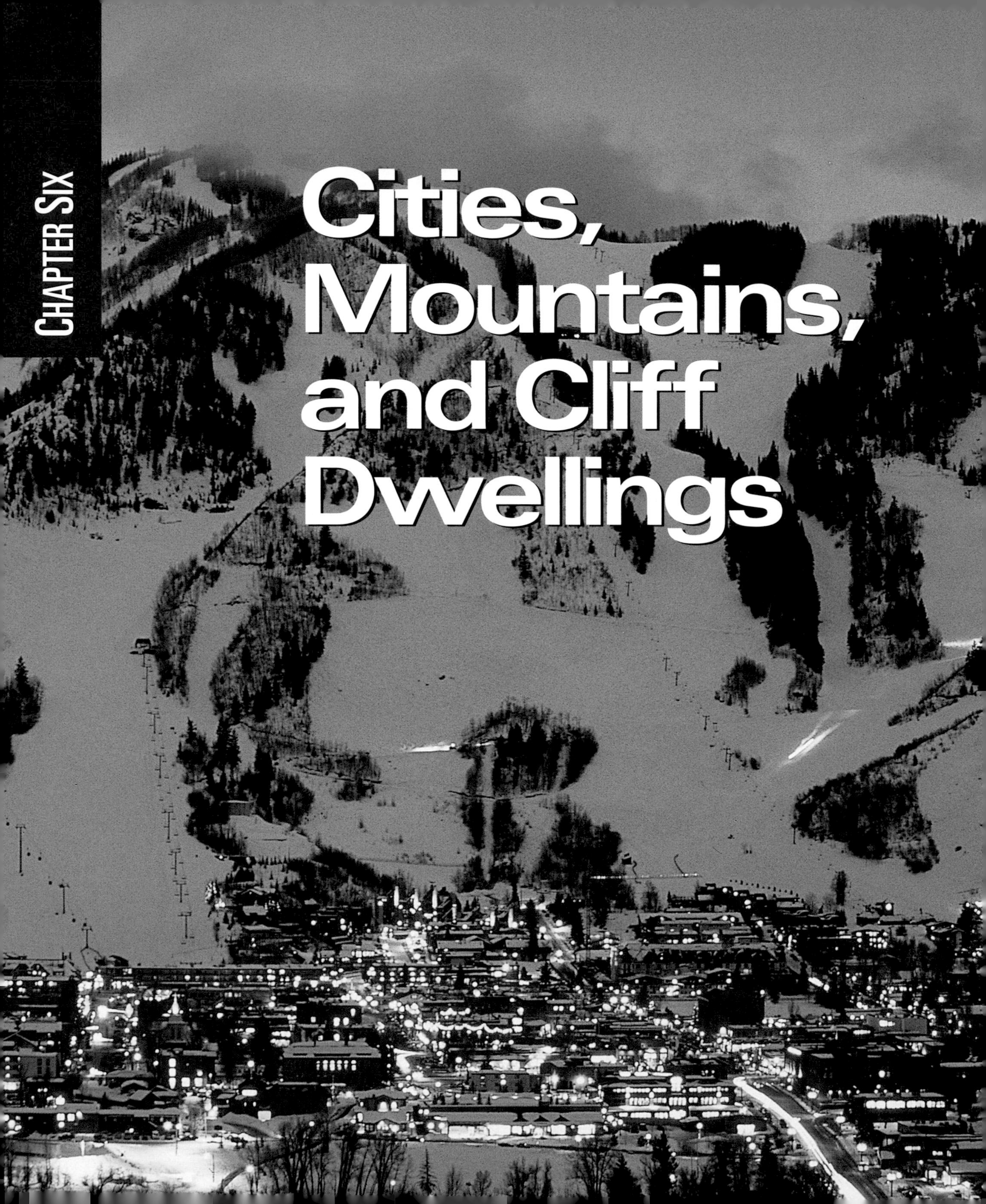

All the major cities of Colorado are located in a line running north to south along the eastern front of the Rocky Mountains. They are, from the north, Fort Collins, Loveland, Longmont, Boulder, Denver, Aurora, Colorado Springs, and Pueblo. Almost half the people in the entire state live in those eight cities.

Interstate 25 runs through or near all of those cities, and that highway is intersected by Interstate 70, which runs east to west, across the High Plains, and through the mountains. At the intersection of those two highways is Denver. Denver has held a Festival of Mountain and Plain for morc than a hundred years. It brings together in celebration the two main aspects of Colorado.

Interstate 70, just outside of Denver

Pueblo

The Colorado State Fair has been held in Pueblo each summer since before Colorado became a state. Pueblo's economy was supported by the mines in the southern part of the state, but it was not a mining town. Instead, because of its location near mountains and on a railway line, it served as a supply center for various mining enterprises. Pueblo has two major areas of preserved Victorian houses that lend it a charm lacking in many plains cities.

Opposite: Aspen at twilight

Pueblo boasts a number of restored Victorian homes.

Wet Mountain Valley lies between the Wet Mountains and the Sangre de Cristo Range. Much of the region is the San Isabel National Forest. The first residents were German immigrants hoping to found a German community, but their central town, Colfax, did not survive. Then, like so much of Colorado, the valley was discovered by prospectors, who found gold in the hills. Today, the valley has ranches and farms, along with a growing tourist business.

A few miles west of Pueblo is Cañon City and its spectacular Royal Gorge. Royal Gorge Bridge, near Cañon City, is the highest suspension bridge in the world. A person standing on the bridge can

The Royal Gorge Bridge is the highest suspension bridge in the world.

peer down 1,053 feet (321 m) to the Arkansas River. Cañon City also has the world's steepest inclined railway, carrying visitors down into the spectacular canyon of the Arkansas River.

Colorado Springs

Colorado Springs was originally the creation of William Jackson Palmer, who created towns to go along with his railroad, the Denver & Rio Grande. Yet, it was the presence of nearby Cripple Creek that turned Colorado Springs into a luxurious place to live.

The gold mines at Cripple Creek yielded the largest amount of gold from any single deposit on Earth, and there's still plenty more where that came from—it just isn't being mined yet. What is seen today at Cripple Creek is not the original town that built up around the mines. That Cripple Creek burned in 1906. The new one, however, was built of stone and brick and has endured.

The Colorado Springs skyline

Fossils of palm trees and other plants and animals are featured at the Florissant Fossil Beds National Monument.

Near Cripple Creek is the Florissant Fossil Beds National Monument. The fossils of palm trees and various tropical plants and animals were imprinted when volcanoes erupted about 36 million years ago. One such sight consists of trunks of giant redwoodlike trees turned to stone.

Colorado Springs got its own gold out of Cripple Creek with the construction of the luxurious Broadmoor Hotel in 1918 by a wealthy mining investor. For many years, the ice-skating rink at the Broadmoor was the U.S. Olympic figure skating training center. In recent years, a new rink has been built, and the World Figure Skating Hall of Fame is located nearby. The May Natural History Museum in Colorado Springs has one of the world's great collections of invertebrates, even gigantic insects from tropical jungles. ProRodeo Hall of Fame and Museum of the American Cowboy are in Colorado Springs. Several rodeo events are held each year in the city, including a "Little Britches" event for young riders.

On Cheyenne Mountain outside of town is the Will Rogers Shrine of the Sun. Will Rogers was an entertainer and humorist of the 1920s and 1930s who is perhaps best known for one gentle line: "I never met a man I didn't like."

Within Colorado Springs is the amazing Garden of the Gods. This park features odd-shaped monoliths, or stones, that are called earth pillars by geologists. They are large rocks on slopes that are left exposed when rain washes away the lighter-weight material around them. Some of the vertical sandstone rocks stand 330 feet (100 m) tall. It's tempting to use them for rock climbing, but that's not allowed.

The Garden of the Gods is made of land forms called earth pillars.

The city is the national and international headquarters of many different organizations. They vary from the U.S. government's North American Aerospace Defense Command to a number of church groups.

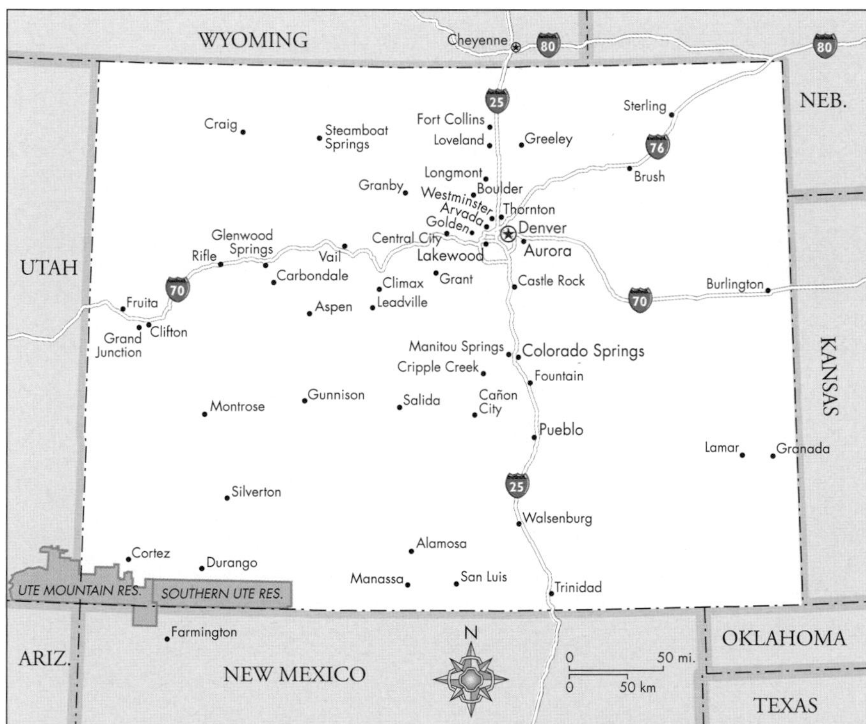

Colorado's cities and interstates

The U.S. Air Force Academy chapel

The U.S. Air Force Academy located near Colorado Springs has an A-shaped chapel that is world famous. The academy occupies an area of more than 25 square miles (65 sq km). The students learn to fly light aircraft there, but they do not fly the big Air Force jets among the mountains.

Pikes Peak, everybody's destination in days of old and now, is located just west of downtown Colorado Springs. On the way is Manitou Cliff Dwellings, a forty-room pueblo where the Anasazi lived about A.D. 1200. Most such pueblos are in the western part of the state. Like a modern version of a cliff dwelling is Miramont Castle, a fantasy building featuring nine different styles of architecture. Built in 1895 by a French priest, it is now a museum. At the foot of Pikes Peak is the town of North Pole. You can guess when the town's post office is the busiest! The nation's second-oldest car race is held on Pikes Peak Highway. The vehicles have to make 156 turns during the 12.4 miles (20 km) of the race, which is held on the Fourth of July. In August, a marathon is run up and down the steep mountain for those hardy enough to do it.

Leadville

Near Grant, on the way from Denver to Leadville, is Mount Evans, which is 14,260 feet (4,346 m) high. It has the highest paved road

Manitou Cliff Dwellings, a forty-room pueblo in which the Anasazi lived

in North America. Leadville forms the third point of a triangle with Colorado Springs and Denver. It is a prime example of what happened to mining towns.

In 1860, a mining camp called Oro City was established, and the area began to boom. When ore was discovered 2 miles (3.2 km) along the mountain track, the miners followed it and started a new camp, Leadville, which quickly grew larger than Oro City. In 1880, the U.S. Census showed that Leadville officially had a population of almost 15,000, but it was probably closer to 24,000. Within another ten years, the population had dropped to 5,500; ten years later, it was back up to 13,000. Then it dwindled until the 1930s, when molybdenum ore was discovered nearby. Molybde-

Checking Their Teeth

Frederick Sumter McKay, a Colorado Springs dentist, reported in 1908 that the people who drank the water in his city had few cavities. But he had to admit that he didn't know why.

It was not until 1931 that scientists identified fluorides as the chemicals in the water that helped strengthen tooth enamel. Since then, most municipalities in the United States have added fluorides to their water supplies. Individuals obtain even more by using fluoridated toothpaste. ■

The Ballad of Baby Doe

Prominent among the residents of Leadville was Horace A. W. Tabor. Originally the owner of a general store in the town, he "grubstaked" (financially supported) two men who soon discovered silver. Tabor became immensely wealthy. He shocked the other upright miners and Denverites when he divorced his wife, Augusta, to marry young Elizabeth McCourt Doe, called Baby Doe.

As Leadville and its mining business shrank, so did Tabor's fortune. He died penniless in 1899 but not before telling Baby Doe to "hang on to the Matchless," convinced that the mine would someday bring her wealth. Baby Doe Tabor lived in a shack outside the Matchless mine for thirty-six years before freezing to death one winter night.

In 1956, an opera called *The Ballad of Baby Doe,* by Douglas Moore and John LaTouche, had its world premiere at the music festival held in the beautiful old opera house of nearby Central City. Baby Doe's tumbledown shack (above) is a tourist attraction. ■

num was useful in strengthening and hardening steel. Technology, however, had kept the need for people to work the mines low, and Leadville never recovered its larger population.

Oro City was a mining camp founded in 1860.

Golden

Near Golden, on Lookout Mountain, are the grave of and a museum dedicated to Buffalo Bill Cody. Cody earned his nickname when he hunted buffalo to feed the railway workers who were building the Kansas Pacific Railway after the Civil War. He served as an Indian scout for the U.S. Cavalry and helped them defeat the Cheyenne in the 1869 Battle of Summit Springs near the village of Atwood in northeastern Colorado. Buffalo Bill went on to become one of the great international entertainers, giving Wild West shows, featuring Annie Oakley, throughout the world.

Jolly Rancher Candy Company began in Golden in the 1950s and moved to Wheat Ridge in 1951. Jolly Rancher became popular with people all over the nation because the small square hard candies lasted longer than most and were less expensive.

Into the Mountains

Loveland Pass, located at 11,992 feet (3,655 m), was the main road through the mountains for car traffic until the Eisenhower Memorial Tunnel and E. Johnson Memorial Tunnel were blasted

Buffalo Bill Cody's grave on Lookout Mountain

through the mountains near Idaho Springs. These tunnels are located about 3,000 feet (914 m) lower than the pass.

Draped across the Continental Divide is the most popular of tourist destinations in Colorado, Rocky Mountain National Park. Most people visiting the park go to Estes Park, located in the Front Range by Longs Peak. Homesteaded by the Estes family in the 1860s, its beauty was publicized by William Byers of the *Rocky Mountain News*. An Irish nobleman, Lord Dunraven, purchased the entire area in the 1870s and turned it into his private hunting estate. Because he didn't own parts of it legally, would-be settlers gradually challenged his rights to the land. Then F. O.

Rail to the Top

The only way to reach the top of Pikes Peak in the early days of tourism was by mule. The trip took two days and was taken only by the most devoted fans of heights. In the mid-1880s, Zalmon Simmons made the trip but was certain there must be a better way to get to the top.

Simmons was staying in Manitou Springs when he was presented with the idea of building a railroad to the top of Pikes Peak. He funded the idea with earnings from his mattress business, and the Manitou & Pikes Peak Cog Railway Company made its first ascent on June 30, 1891.

The cog railway was invented in New Hampshire but is used primarily in Switzerland. Instead of depending on the wheels sticking to a track, the cog railway has a gear between the rails that meshes with a cog (like the tooth on a gear) on the trail. It can climb much steeper grades than a regular train.

Hiking is popular within Rocky Mountain National Park.

Stanley of the early "Stanley Steamer" automobile bought parts of it. Rocky Mountain National Park was created in 1915 at the urging of natural history writer Enos A. Mills.

The park covers 265,727 acres (107,536 ha) and includes some of the most spectacular mountain scenery of North America. Longs Peak itself was named for Stephen Long, leader of the expedition that called eastern Colorado a "great desert." It is 14,255 feet (4,345 m) high and is also famous for its East Face, which has a sheer drop of 1,675 feet (511 m). Trail Ridge Road out of Rocky Mountain National Park is the highest continuously paved road in the United States.

Springtime in Aspen

Across the Great Divide

About 100 miles (161 km) from Denver on the western side of the Continental Divide is Aspen. Located on the Roaring Fork River at 7,800 feet (2,377 m), it is surrounded by the White River National Forest. Although Aspen is most famous for its winter skiing, it is a popular summer destination, too, especially because of the Aspen Music Festival.

Founded by silver prospectors in 1879 as Ute City, Aspen was too isolated to thrive until a smelting (ore separation) plant was built four years later. Soon it had a population of 10,000 and even an opera house. It seemed that nothing could stop Aspen—except running out of silver. After the price supports were removed from silver, Aspen nearly became a ghost town. Its population shrank to about 700.

Aspen's revival began in 1936 when workers for the WPA (Works Progress Administration; after 1939, Works Projects Administration) built a ski lift. Then, during World War II, Aspen was used to train volunteers for fighting in snow-covered mountains. Most of these skiers ended up serving in the mountains of northern Italy, and many of them returned to Aspen after the war.

Chicago businessman Walter Paepcke started the Aspen Institute for Humanistic Studies and a music festival in the remote location in 1949. The institute is a program of lectures and discussions on many different subjects to which people come from all over the world. Thus, the town started growing again.

Today, Aspen is a world-class ski facility, with more ski lifts than any other ski area in the world. There are four major ski areas in the region: Snowmass, Aspen Highlands, Tiehack, and Aspen Mountain. The mountains are dotted with beautiful homes, luxury vacation condominiums, and top-quality restaurants. Many of Aspen's original mining-era buildings have been remodeled and add Victorian charm to the very modern community.

The highest pass in the world that is usable by automobiles is located near Aspen. Called Independence Pass, it is at an elevation of 12,095 feet (3,687 m).

Vail's population grows on winter weekends.

Ski Communities

Although Aspen is grander than many ski communities, it is fairly typical of several such places in the Colorado Rockies. They combine incredible ski facilities, beautiful countryside, awe-inspiring mountains, historically preserved buildings, and unique history. Among these ski-country communities are Vail, Glenwood Springs, Steamboat Springs, and Breckenridge. Each has its own unique characteristics. Many of them have summer music and theater festivals.

Vail is a small mountainside community that becomes overpopulated on weekends, surging from its normal population of 7,000 to more than 35,000. Traffic problems used to plague residents and visitors alike on

Tourists enjoy the steaming waters of Glenwood Springs.

weekends until the town put in traffic roundabouts. On roundabouts, cars move right onto a circular road. When they reach the street they want, they turn off. The traffic on the roundabout itself never stops, and there are fewer accidents than at traffic lights. Other cities in Colorado are considering the same kind of traffic device to cure their weekend problems.

The same kind of traffic problems hit Aspen and Glenwood Springs. Though these towns are only 44 miles (71 km) apart, often it takes more than two hours to drive the distance because of congestion on a two-lane highway. These towns are planning to build Roaring Fork Valley Rail by 2010. It will be a light-rail line, which means that it does not require a heavy locomotive as long-distance trains do.

The Vail area was made famous by the photographs of William Henry Jackson, taken in the 1870s. Vail was not originally a mining area; rather, its visitors came mostly for hunting. A World War II veteran who had trained for wartime skiing in the area turned Vail into a resort.

The Breckenridge area in Summit County includes four ski areas: Arapahoe Basin, Keystone, Copper Mountain, and Breckenridge itself. Breckenridge was a gold-mining community where the world's largest gold nugget was found by miner Tom Groves. It weighed in at 13 pounds (5.9 kg). The town was named for the vice president of the United States, but when the residents learned that John C. Breckinridge was a supporter of the Confederacy during the Civil War, they changed the spelling of the town's name. Today, Breckenridge is the center of the snowboarding world.

The ski area of Winter Park offers a bonus for disabled people who want to ski. Since 1980, the area has supported a major program of skiing for the blind and the physically and mentally challenged. This is the largest program of its kind, involving hundreds of volunteers throughout the winter.

A 12-mile (19-km) stretch of highway going through Glenwood Canyon near Glenwood Springs took thirteen years to build because the road had to go through a narrow hard-rock canyon with 1,800-foot (548-m) walls. Part of the highway goes through a tunnel. A spectacular 20-mile (32-km) bike path runs along the Colorado River in sight of the highway.

The San Juan Mountains were settled by Hispanic people.

South and West

A very different kind of history from that of "Anglo" prospectors can be found in San Luis Valley between the Sangre de Cristo Mountains and the San Juans. This region was settled by Hispanic people coming northward from Mexico and New Mexico.

At the center of the valley is the town of Alamosa, a thriving market center. The town of San Luis is Colorado's oldest town, founded in 1851. Much of the valley is watered by the Rio Grande. Like the people who live on the same river farther south forming the border between Texas and Mexico, San Luis residents celebrate Mexican Independence Day in September. Cinco de Mayo festivals honor Mexico's victory against the French on May 5, 1862.

On the other side of the San Juan Mountains are the two Ute Indian reservations. Between them lies Mesa Verde National Park. This region of Anasazi cliff dwellings has been recognized internationally as one of the World Heritage Cultural Sites that must be preserved.

Hovenweep National Monument is a 785-acre (318-ha) area straddling the border of southwestern Colorado and southeastern Utah. It includes the ruins of six prehistoric pueblo sites. The name derives from a Ute word meaning "deserted valley." Unlike the people of Mesa Verde, the Anasazi who lived in the Hovenweep region built stone towers. One tower, called Hovenweep Castle, has walls 20 feet (6 m) high.

Durango, north of the Southern Ute Reservation, is a town of the Wild West. Surrounded by the San Juan National Forest, it is located in the valley of the Animas River. The river's full name is El Río de las Animas Perdidas, which means "The River of Lost Souls." Near Durango is a ski center for people who aren't quite ready to challenge the Rockies.

One of the delights of this section of Colorado is a 45-mile (72-km) ride on the Durango & Silverton Narrow Gauge Railway. Originally part of the Denver & Rio Grande system, Durango & Silverton was abandoned in the 1960s and eventually bought by a Florida businessman. He revived the railway, which carries pas-

A ride on the Durango & Silverton Narrow Gauge Railway attracts many tourists to the area.

sengers on a hair-raising and spectacular journey on cliffs overlooking the Animas River. The end of the line is Silverton, an almost ghost-town mining community like those around Denver.

Not far from Silverton, deep in the mountains, is Colorado's newest beautiful ski area, Telluride. The remoteness of Telluride kept it from becoming a popular destination until the mid-1980s, when an airport was built nearby. Telluride lovers won't allow major resorts to overwhelm their historically beautiful small town, which has about 2,000 full-time residents. Instead, they sent developers to an elevation of 10,000 feet (3,048 m) above the

A bird's-eye view of Telluride's ski runs

town to create Mountain Village. The town below and the village above are connected by a "commuter system" of cable cars, each carrying six passengers.

The heart of the region called the Western Slope is Grand Junction, which lies in the valley formed by the junction of the Colorado and Gunnison Rivers. Near Grand Junction is Colorado National Monument, established in 1911. It is a natural area of canyons along a section of the Grand Valley of the Colorado River. Huge red sandstone pinnacles, or monoliths, jut from the earth in spectacular array.

Grand Mesa in Mesa and Delta Counties has nearly three hundred lakes. Fly-fishing is immensely popular. Rainbow trout, in particular, are a challenge to land and are good eating.

The area around the Green River has a special rock formation called oil shale. The rocks contain an organic fluid similar to petroleum. Called kerogen, this material has been likened to "young" or "immature" petroleum. Chunks of the rock itself can be burned as fuel, but geologists want to mine the oil shale and wring the kerogen out of it. So far, the process is too expensive to use, but when the world runs out of petroleum resources, Colorado's oil shale might be one solution.

Western Colorado has been described as still being frontier country because its population per square mile is so low. Most of the residents—especially ranchers—are happy to have it that way.

Chapter Seven

Mile-High Government

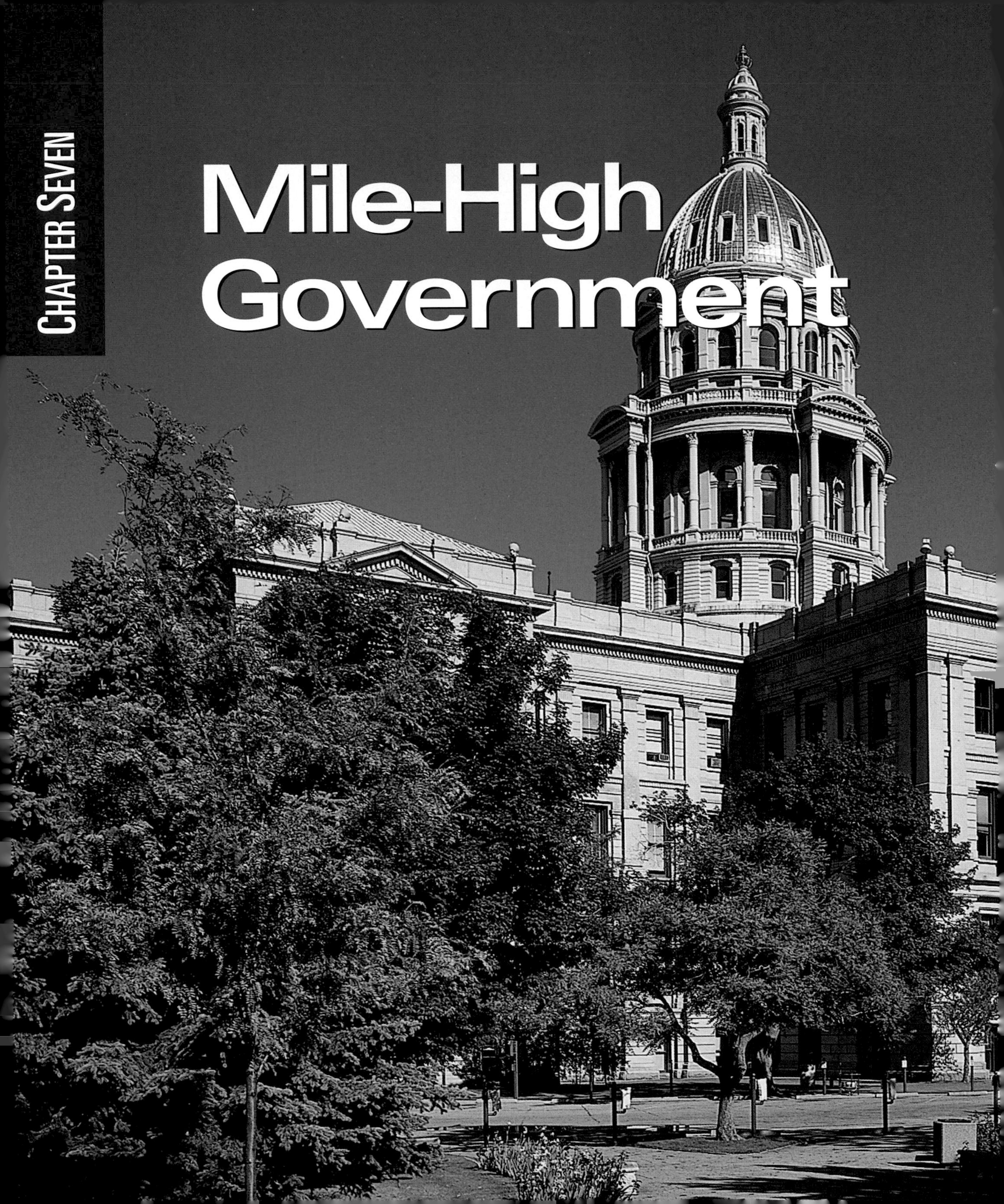

Since its beginning in 1858, Denver has grown into a major city.

James William Denver was a traveling man. Originally a Virginian, Denver fought in the Mexican War with a military company from Missouri. After the war, he went to California where he served as a state senator and California's secretary of state before being elected to the U.S. House of Representatives.

President James Buchanan appointed Denver to be Commissioner of Indian Affairs in 1857 and then territorial governor of Kansas the following year. That was no easy job because Kansas was the center of conflict between people who wanted to end slavery and those who wanted Kansas to be a slave state.

At the time gold was discovered at Cherry Creek in 1858, parts of Colorado were included in Kansas Territory. The miners who decided to settle on the north bank of the creek named their new town for James Denver.

Denver City wasn't alone on Cherry Creek, however. Other miners had begun a camp they called Auraria. Though they were competitors, the two towns cooperated with each other, and in 1860, they merged as Denver.

Opposite: The Colorado State Capitol in Denver

The City That Shouldn't Have Happened

A local historian in the Denver area wrote, "Denver is a city that probably shouldn't have happened." He meant that when it was started in 1858, it didn't have any of the benefits that make a city prosper. It had little water and few trees. It was not near any large city—or even a town. And, to make matters worse, it was in Indian Country.

Then why did Denver thrive? Newcomers were stunned by the magnificent sight of the Front Range and didn't want to leave. The city's location allowed its people to take advantage of both the agriculture on the Great Plains and the mines of the nearby mountains. Add in the fact that Colorado has even more days of sunshine each year than California, and people found it hard to leave.

The *Rocky Mountain News* began publishing on April 23, 1859. The editor and owner was William Byers. It was mostly through his efforts that Denver became the center of the state and eventually the capital. Less than two years after the gold rush had started, Byers was optimistically predicting that Denver would become the "largest inland city on the American continent." The paper is still published today, but Byers was a bit too hopeful. While Denver is the largest city in Colorado, many cities in the Midwest are larger.

The first Territorial Legislative Assembly meeting in Denver in 1861 named Colorado City the capital of the territory. Even so, within months, the capital was moved to Golden City. Although Denver burned to the ground in 1863, it was rebuilt quickly, and in 1867, it was named the capital of the state. Denver has remained the capital and by far the largest city.

Colorado Government

The state capitol, in the center of the city, was begun in 1886. It took twenty-two years to build. It looks rather like the U.S. Capitol in Washington, D.C., but its dome is covered with gold leaf.

The constitution that governs Colorado is the same one that was approved by Colorado voters back in 1876.

Colorado's State Government

Executive Branch

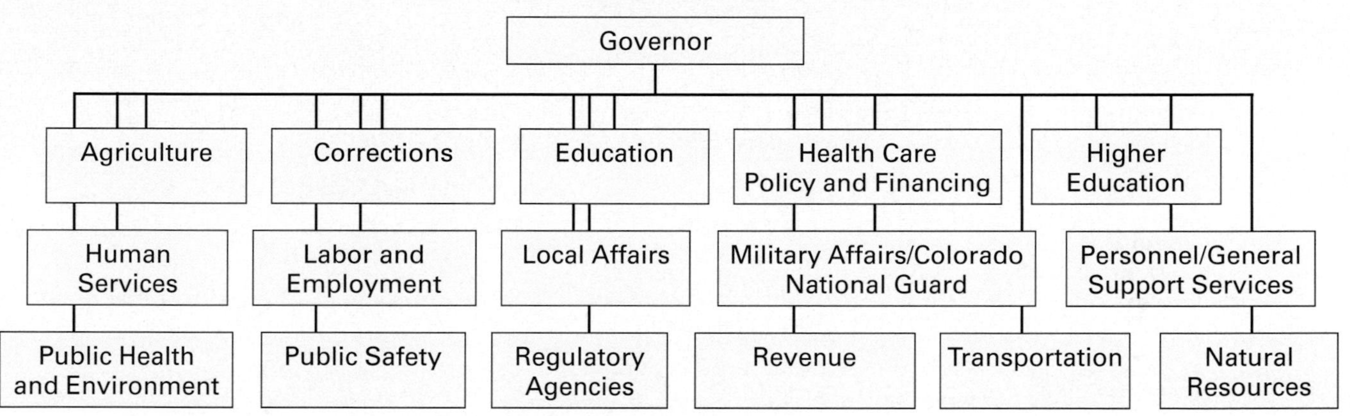

Legislative Branch

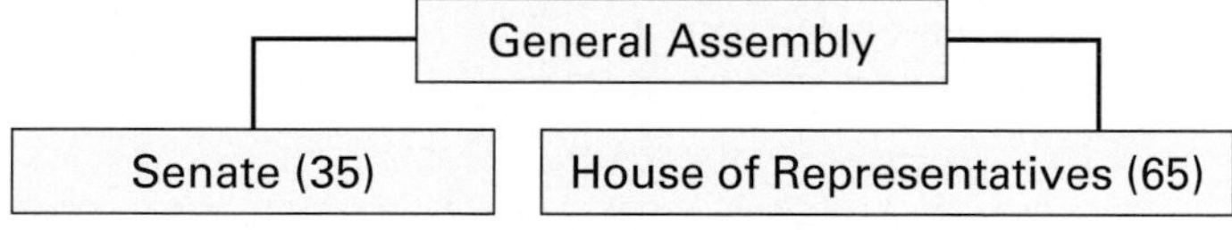

Judicial Branch

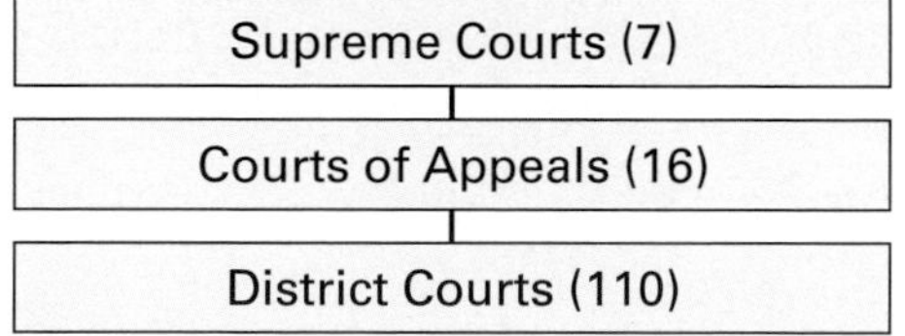

The Colorado State Flag

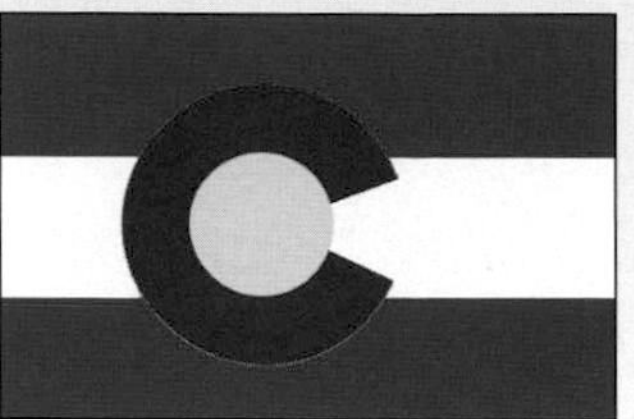

The Colorado state flag consists of three alternate stripes of equal width. The two outer stripes are a deep blue and the inner stripe is white. A red "C" is slightly off-center and to the left in the middle of the flag. Andrew Carlisle Johnson designed the flag in 1911. On February 28, 1929, the General Assembly stipulated the exact colors of the blue and red of the flag. The exact placement of the "C" was set by legislation signed on March 31, 1964.

Colorado's State Symbols

State animal: Rocky Mountain bighorn sheep On May 1, 1961, the General Assembly adopted the Rocky Mountain bighorn sheep as the state's official animal. These sheep are found only in the Rocky Mountains and usually live above the timberline. These large animals are especially known for their agility and sense of balance.

State bird: Lark bunting The lark bunting is a migratory bird that arrives in Colorado in April and returns south again in September. The male is black with white wing patches and the female is a gray brown. In winter, the males change color and are also a gray brown. The General Assembly adopted the lark bunting as the state bird on April 29, 1931.

State fish: Greenback cutthroat trout The greenback cutthroat trout was, at one time, common in many of Colorado's streams and creeks. With the expansion of mining and other industrial activities, the greenback eventually became rare. During the 1980s, environmentalists feared that the fish was extinct. In the early 1990s, small populations of the fish were found in isolated streams, and efforts have begun to repopulate the state's waterways.

State flower: Rocky Mountain columbine The white and lavender Rocky Mountain columbine (opposite) became the state flower on April 4, 1899, by an act of the General Assembly. This delicate flower is protected throughout the state, and it is illegal to pick more than twenty-five in any one day.

State folk dance: Square dance This American folk dance is similar to country and folk dances from England and France. It was formally adopted as the state folk dance on March 16, 1992.

State fossil: Stegosaurus This dinosaur was common in what is now called Colorado more than 150 million years ago. Only six skeletons of the Stegosaurus are on public display, one of which is at the Museum of Natural History in Denver. This fossil was discovered in January 1980 by a group of students from Cañon City High School. The Stegosaurus was designated state fossil on April 28, 1982.

State gemstone: Aquamarine Colorado contains some of the finest known mines of aquamarines in the world. These pale blue to deep green gemstones range in size from very small to about 2.5 inches (6 cm) in length. The aquamarine was chosen as the state gemstone by an act of the General Assembly on April 30, 1971.

State grass: Blue grama grass This grass is native to Colorado, growing wild on both sides of the Continental Divide. The General Assembly adopted blue grama grass as the official state grass on May 20, 1987.

State insect: Colorado hairstreak butterfly This 2-inch-(5-cm) wide butterfly has purple wings with black borders and orange accents in the corners and blue on the underside. The Colorado hairstreak lives at elevations of about 6,500 to 7,500 feet (1,981 to 2,286 m) and lives in the unusual habitat of the scrub oak. It was adopted as state insect on April 17, 1996.

State tree: Colorado blue spruce The Colorado blue spruce was first discovered on Pikes Peak by a botanist named C. C. Parry in 1862. This tree is now widely known for its silver-blue needles and fine symmetrical shape. It was adopted as the state tree by the General Assembly on March 7, 1939. ■

Colorado's State Song
"Where the Columbines Grow"

Words and music by A. J. Flynn

Where the snowy peaks gleam
in the moonlight,
Above the dark forests of pine,
And the wild foaming waters
dash onward
Towards land where the tropic
stars shine;
Where the scream of the bold
mountain eagle,
Responds to the notes of the
dove,
Is the purple robed West, the
land that is best,
The pioneer land that we love.

Chorus:
'Tis the land where the
columbines grow,
Over-looking the plains far
below,
While the cool summer breeze
in the evergreen trees
Softly sings where the
columbines grow.

The bison is gone from the
upland,
The deer from the canyon has
fled,
The home of the wolf is
deserted,
The antelope moans for his
dead,
The war whoop re-echoes no
longer
The Indian's only a name,
And the nymphs of the grove
in their loneliness rove,
But the columbine blooms just
the same.

(Chorus)

Let the violet brighten the
brookside,
In sunlight of earlier spring,
Let the clover bedeck the green
meadow,
In days when the orioles sing,
Let the goldenrod herald the
autumn,
But under the midsummer sky,
In its fair Western home, may
the columbine bloom
Till our great mountain rivers
run dry.

(Chorus)

As are the governments of most states, Colorado's government is patterned after the U.S. federal government. At the top the executive branch is the governor. There are sixteen departments in the executive branch, including agriculture, human services, military affairs and the Colorado National Guard, and natural resources.

Colorado's Governors

Name	Party	Term	Name	Party	Term
John L. Routt	Rep.	1876–1879	Julius C. Gunter	Dem.	1917–1919
Frederick W. Pitkin	Rep.	1879–1883	Oliver H. Shoup	Rep.	1919–1923
James B. Grant	Dem.	1883–1885	William E. Sweet	Dem.	1923–1925
Benjamin H. Eaton	Rep.	1885–1887	Clarence J. Morley	Rep.	1925–1927
Alva Adams	Dem.	1887–1889	William H. Adams	Dem.	1927–1933
Job A. Cooper	Rep.	1889–1891	Edwin C. Johnson	Dem.	1933–1937
John L. Routt	Rep.	1891–1893	Raymond H. Talbot	Dem.	1937
Davis H. Waite	Pop.	1893–1895	Teller Ammons	Dem.	1937–1939
Albert W. McIntire	Rep.	1895–1897	Ralph L. Carr	Rep.	1939–1943
Alva Adams	Dem.	1897–1899	John C. Vivian	Rep.	1943–1947
Charles S. Thomas	Dem.	1899–1901	W. Lee Knous	Dem.	1947–1950
James B. Orman	Dem.	1901–1903	Walter W. Johnson	Dem.	1950–1951
James H. Peabody	Rep.	1903–1905	Daniel J. J. Thornton	Rep.	1951–1955
Alva Adams	Dem.	1905	Edwin C. Johnson	Dem.	1955–1957
James H. Peabody	Rep.	1905	Stephen L. R. McNichols	Dem.	1957–1963
Jesse F. McDonald	Rep.	1905–1907	John A. Love	Rep.	1963–1973
Henry A. Buchtel	Rep.	1907–1909	John D. Vanderhoof	Rep.	1973–1975
John F. Shafroth	Dem.	1909–1913	Richard D. Lamm	Dem.	1975–1987
Elias M. Ammons	Dem.	1913–1915	Roy Romer	Dem.	1987–1999
George A. Carlson	Rep.	1915–1917	William Owens	Rep.	1999–

The state legislature is called the General Assembly. It is divided into two branches. The upper house, or Senate, has thirty-five members. The lower house, or House of Representatives, has sixty-five members. The major responsibility of the General Assembly is to decide how the state's money will be spent.

The judicial branch of government interprets the laws passed by the legislature and includes all the courts from local districts on up. In the twenty-two districts of the state are district courts that

The Colorado legislature in session

include 110 judges, who are appointed to their positions by the governor. Denver also has a juvenile court with three judges and a probate court (handling wills and estates of people who die) with one judge.

Any person involved in a case in a district court can appeal the decision of a district court. Appeals cases are heard by any of sixteen judges on the court of appeals. Finally, the top court, the Colorado supreme court, has seven judges.

The state is divided into sixty-three counties. Denver, El Paso, Arapahoe, and Jefferson are the largest counties—all with populations around 500,000. These counties are all part of the highly populated region that extends down to Colorado Springs. San Juan, Mineral, and Hinsdale counties have fewer than a thousand people each.

Patricia Schroeder was elected to Congress in 1973 and served for more than twenty years.

Colorado has sent representatives to Washington under four names. In 1858, Hiram Graham represented the "People of Pikes Peak." The following year, a delegate went from Jefferson Territory. In 1861, Colorado Territory was formed, and for fifteen years sent territorial delegates to Washington. Since 1876, two senators and a varying number of representatives have gone to Washington from the state of Colorado.

Today, Colorado sends six people to the U.S. House of Representatives. Patricia Schroeder was the first Colorado woman elected to Congress. She was first elected in 1973 and served for more than

The Only Native American in Congress

Ben Nighthorse Campbell was born in California, where he spent most of his youth in foster homes because his three-quarter Cheyenne father and Portuguese mother were unable to take care of him. After college, he participated in the Olympics as captain of the U.S. judo team.

Now a resident of Ignacio, Campbell is a jewelry designer and rancher. Concerned about Colorado's status in the United States, he was elected to a seat in the U.S. House of Representatives in 1986. Six years later, Campbell was elected to represent the state in the U.S. Senate.

Ben Campbell spent most of his political career as a Democrat, but in 1995, he switched to the Republican party. In 1998, he was reelected to the Senate.

He still designs Native American jewelry, breeds champion quarter horses, and rides his motorcycle—all while representing Colorado, rural living, and Native Americans. ■

twenty years. Since her first election, several women from Colorado have served in Congress.

The Federal Government

When Colorado was created, it was comprised of land that belonged to the U.S. government. Today, the U.S. government still controls more than a third of Colorado's land, usually in very confusing ways. Almost two dozen different government agencies are involved in this control. The largest part of the state—the twelve national forests and two national grasslands—is administered by the U.S. Forest Service.

North of Denver is the Rocky Mountain Arsenal, a huge open area that was used during and after World War II by the federal government as a construction and test site for chemical weapons. When the government stopped using it, the grounds were found to be terribly contaminated with poisonous wastes. The cleanup will

The Mesa Verde National Park is run by the National Park Service.

probably not be completed for years, but in the meantime, a wealth of wildlife has made the arsenal lands home, apparently unbothered by the toxic wastes. It is now a national wildlife refuge.

The federal Bureau of Land Management controls the number of ranchers that may use federal land for grazing their cattle. That agency also plays a major role in the projects that move water around the state. The National Park Service administers the two national parks: Mesa Verde and Rocky Mountain.

The U.S. Air Force Academy was created by President Dwight Eisenhower in 1954. The first class of cadets met temporarily at Denver's Lowry Air Force Base but moved into their new quarters near Colorado Springs in the autumn of 1958.

When a U.S. Air Force Base in Denver closed, a huge hangar where B-52 bombers had been worked on was left empty. In 1997, Big Bear Ice Arena opened inside the hangar. It includes two rinks large enough to hold National Hockey League games. The developers of the rink envision it as the centerpiece of a major sports complex that will include several athletic fields.

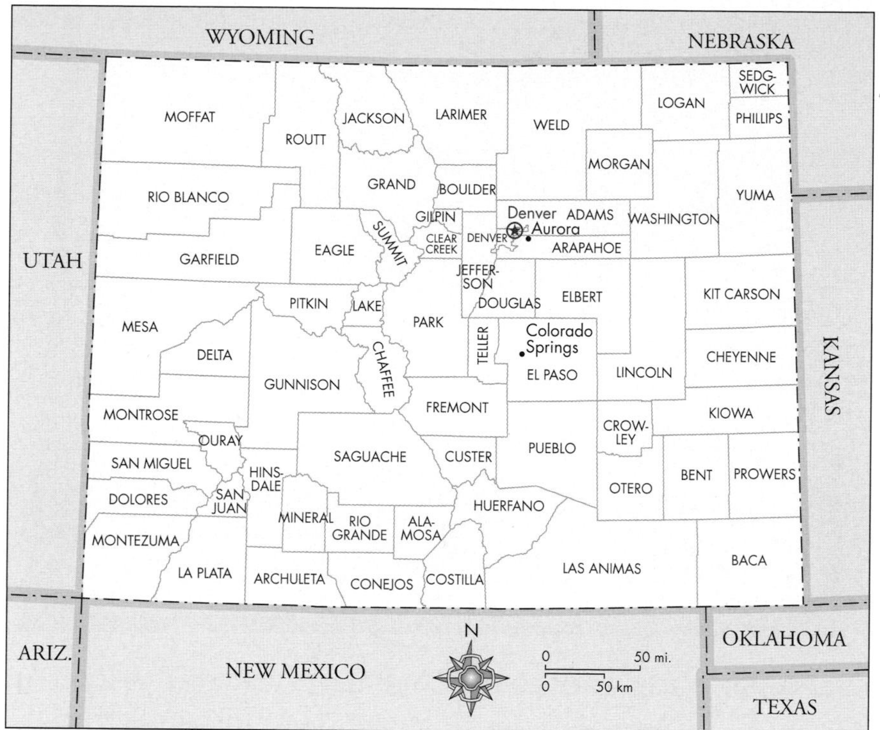

Colorado's counties

The Metropolitan Denver Area

Denver is both a city and a county, so its government combines the functions of both. The original city limits were 10 miles (16 km) west of where the Rocky Mountains start, but since the 1950s the city and its suburbs have crept into the mountains.

Denver proudly calls itself the Mile-High City and posts signs around the city giving its elevation as 5,280 feet (1,609 m). In reality, though, the city occupies many different elevations. Parts of the city are higher than a mile, and a few parts are less. A mile sounds high, but Denver is 2 miles (3 km) lower in elevation than some of the lofty peaks of the nearby mountains.

The South Platte River runs through the city and eventually flows into Nebraska. In recent years, the riverfront has been cleaned up and beautiful walkways installed.

For several years after gold began to pour out of the Colorado mountains, privately produced gold coins were made in Denver.

Denver's "mountains" of skyscrapers lie about 10 miles (16 km) east of the Rocky Mountains.

One company circulated about $3 million in gold coins before the federal government stopped such coin-making in 1861. Since 1906, Denver has had a mint (a coin-making factory) for the U.S. government. If you look closely at a dime, you may see a small *D* by the date. That shows that the coin was minted in Denver.

Downtown and Its People

Like many cities across the United States, Denver passed laws that stopped the segregation of people of different races or heritages into isolated sections of the city. Also as in numerous cities, many people began to move to the suburbs, and the inner, older city began to deteriorate. Parts of Denver have recently been designated as "enterprise zones." If businesses move into an enterprise zone or work to improve it, they get special tax benefits.

In 1908, Denver passed a law requiring that no buildings be high enough to block the view of the mountains from the capital. In effect, that meant no building could be higher than twelve stories. While other cities built many skyscrapers, Denver did not change its law until the 1960s. Since then, new skyscrapers in the downtown area have attracted businesses, leaving other parts of the downtown to deteriorate.

In the area called Lower Downtown (shortened to "LoDo"), run-down old buildings are being bought and refurbished. Many shops and restaurants are bringing people to the area again. The area called the Golden Triangle is also being redeveloped to make a friendly livable neighborhood right near the main downtown attractions and workplaces.

Since the 1960s, Denver has built many skyscrapers.

Downtown Denver has acquired a very international flavor in recent years. Hispanics have always played an important part in Denver, and they even have a Greater Denver Hispanic Guide on the Internet. In addition to letting people know about Spanish-speaking doctors, dentists, restaurants, and so on, the site provides a history of some of the Hispanic nations from which Denver's Hispanic residents originated. The Hispanic community celebrates with a Cinco de Mayo ("May Fifth") festival, which was the date of a battle in Mexico against French forces in 1862.

Sakura Square in Denver is centered around a Buddhist temple. The area has a Japanese flavor and holds a Japanese festival each year. In addition, there is a Japanese Garden in the famed Denver Botanic Gardens. Immigrants from other Asian countries such as Vietnam and Korea have brought some of their original cultures to Denver.

Denver's Hispanic Mayor

Originally from Texas, Federico Peña moved to Denver as a young man to work as a lawyer. He was elected to the state legislature as a Democrat in 1979, and four years later was elected mayor of Denver by asking Denverites to "imagine a great city." Then he set about trying to build one.

Peña served as mayor from 1983 to 1991. He was responsible for getting the approvals for the new Denver International Airport and put a great deal of work into improving areas of Denver that were deteriorating. In 1991, President Clinton named Peña to his cabinet. He first served as Secretary of Transportation and then as Secretary of Energy. ■

African-Americans have lived in Denver from the very beginning, when black cowboys left the trail and settled down. Denver's Black American West Museum and Heritage Center calls attention to the fact that many of the cowboys of the Old West were African-Americans.

For two weeks each January, another "ethnic group"—the cowboy—comes to Denver. Real broncos can be seen when the National Western Stock Show and Rodeo comes to town. The largest livestock show in the world, it draws stock breeders and rodeo riders from all over the nation. The January event, which has been held since 1906, draws almost 700,000 visitors and champion rodeo riders to the Denver Coliseum from all over.

Getting To and From Denver

It wasn't until 1927 that Denver could be reached easily by railroads. The Moffat Tunnel was dug under the Continental Divide. Because it was built from one river—Boulder Creek—to another—the head of the Colorado River—the 6.4-mile (10.3-km) tunnel was also used to carry water to the Denver area.

The main terminal of the Denver International Airport

Denver's old Union Station is still used by the "heavy" rail of Amtrak, the national passenger railway system. Denver is now also a hub of "light rail," though. Light-rail lines are short-distance commuter trains that don't require the heavy locomotives of long-distance trains. They are a relatively inexpensive form of mass transportation. The Denver area has had some light rail since 1995. More lines have been approved, which will create a light rail system 120 miles (193 km) long.

Stapleton Airport, named for the longtime mayor of the city, served Denver for many years, but in the 1980s so many people were coming to Colorado that Stapleton became the fourth-busiest airport in the United States. Skiers alone kept the airport busy, and the amount of other business in the region was increasing by leaps and bounds. The old airport had no room to grow.

So, Denver, the state, and the federal government approved a new Denver International Airport (DIA). Its buildings are a series of tentlike peaks that resemble the Rocky Mountains. The DIA has twelve runways and occupies 53 square miles (137 sq km), making it the largest airport used by commercial airlines in the world. The immense project ended up costing almost $5 billion. Most Coloradans, though stunned at the cost, realize that the airport has been built for a future in which Denver will continue to grow as a crossroads for North America.

Chapter Eight

Prospecting for Minerals and Visitors

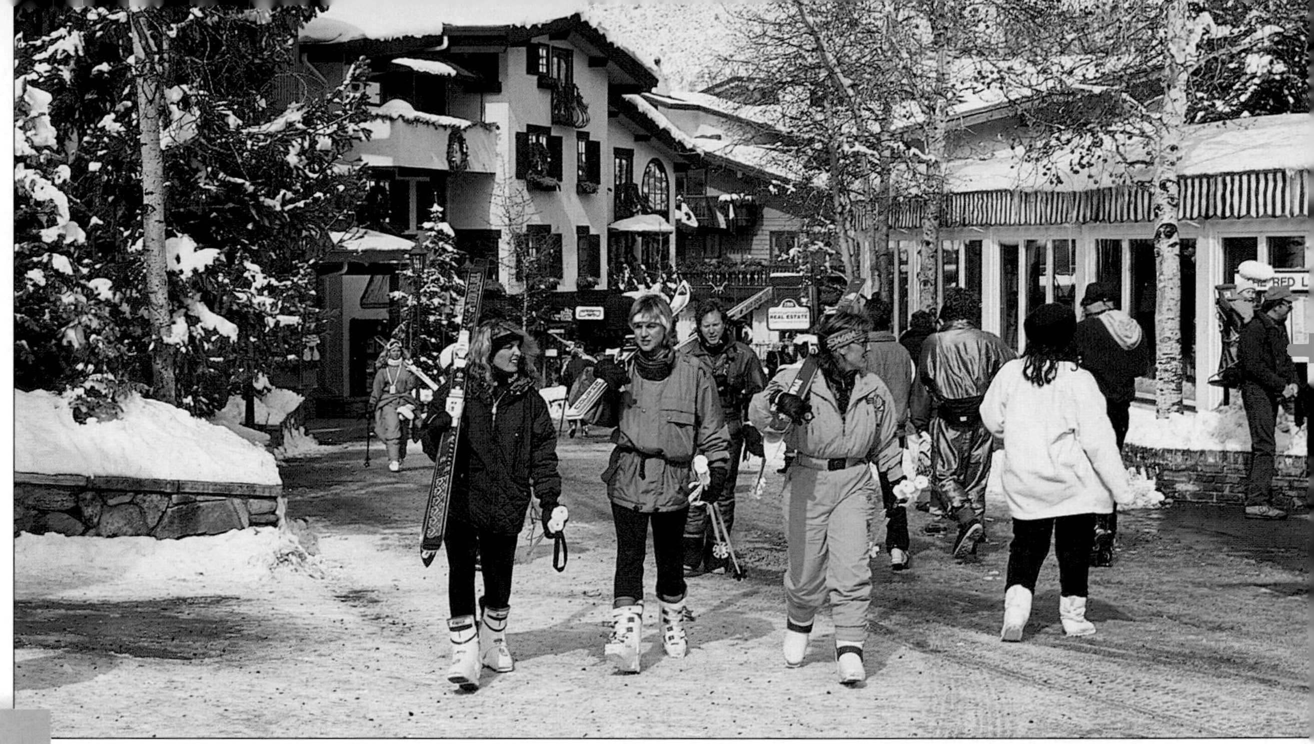

Tourism at Vail and other ski resorts is a major industry in Colorado.

In the early days of statehood, Colorado's promoters—especially the railroads—learned the value of publicity in promoting their state. They had newspaper and magazine articles written glorifying Colorado. Artists came to make sketches that were sold on postcards. Pamphlets were sent around the world to locations from which immigrants might come. These efforts worked to bring the curious to Colorado, and the sheer beauty of the state made them stay.

Nothing has changed. Colorado is a state that takes advantage of its beautiful scenery as well as its natural resources to build a thriving economy. Although mining was the original reason for the state's development, today tourism is Colorado's largest private-sector employer. Only the federal government is larger.

Still Prospecting

Colorado is still a mining state but in a different way than a century ago. At Climax, near the old silver-mining town of Leadville, is the world's largest molybdenum mine. Perched high atop the

Opposite: A ski lift at Steamboat Springs

Climax has the world's largest molybdenum mine.

Continental Divide, the mine is located at more than 13,000 feet (3,962 m). The post office in Climax has been called the highest post office in the United States.

Back in the gold-mining days, the miners had seen the molybdenum ore, but they thought it was lead and ignored it. The molybdenum at Climax was properly identified in 1900, but no uses were known for it for another fifteen years. Today, molybdenum is a very valuable metal used in manufacturing special steels for use where high heat resistance is needed.

Durango was the site of the Smelter Mountain Mill, which processed uranium ore for use in building atomic bombs made at Los Alamos, New Mexico, in the 1940s and 1950s. The processing produced a uranium oxide, called yellowcake. Many Native American workers at the Smelter Mountain Mill became ill and even died because of the radioactive material they handled.

A modern gold rush occurred in the 1970s when the price of gold reached $500 a troy ounce (there are 12 troy ounces to a pound instead of the usual 16). It was once again worthwhile to mine gold that had been left long ago. Such high prices did not last long, however, and neither did the revived gold mines.

Mining of a different kind takes place near Aspen in the Yule

What Colorado Grows, Manufactures, and Mines

Agriculture	Manufacturing	Mining
Beef cattle	Scientific instruments	Petroleum
Corn	Electrical equipment	Coal
Wheat	Printed materials	Natural gas
Milk		
Hay		

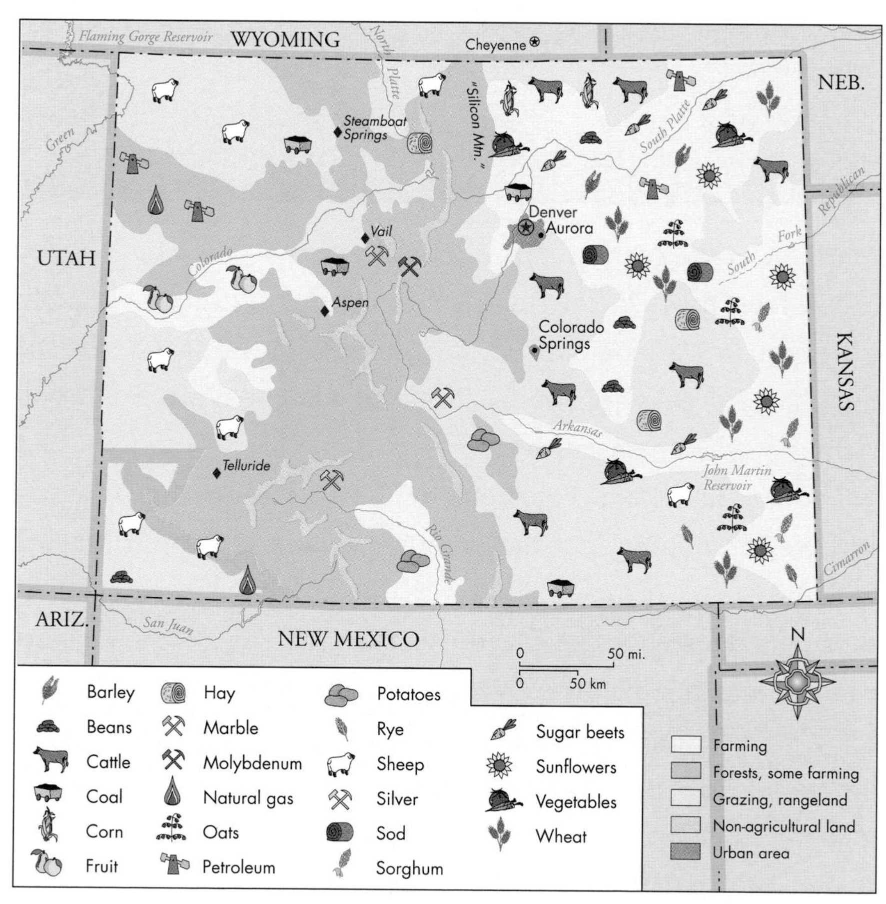

Colorado's natural resources

The Yule Marble Quarry near Aspen

Marble Quarry. A special white marble, called Colorado Yule for Yule Creek, provided the stone for the interior of the great Lincoln Memorial in Washington, D.C. An immense 100-ton solid block of marble from Yule became the Tomb of the Unknown Soldier in Arlington National Cemetery.

Today, less than 3 percent of the Colorado workforce is involved in mining, but the mining industry still contributes a great deal to the economy. Machines do most of the work that used to require hundreds of people. Prospectors still scout the mountains of Colorado, hoping to find valuable mineral deposits no one else has claimed. Many small mountain towns still have residents who are trained to test and measure the amount of gold, silver, or other valuable metal in an ore, but these assayers don't have much work to do nowadays.

Silicon Mountain

In 1997, *Forbes* business magazine predicted that during the coming years four of the twenty-five areas in the United States with the fastest growth in jobs would be in Colorado. The magazine named the four areas: Denver, the Boulder/Longmont region, the Fort Collins/Loveland region, and Colorado Springs. Much of the reason for such anticipated growth is the increasing number of high-technology industries that are contributing to the booming Colorado economy.

A region in California is called the Silicon Valley. It has many jobs in electronics (most of which use the element silicon in their intricate parts). The Front Range area of Colorado has been called Silicon Mountain because of its numerous jobs in high-technology industries. The region is third behind the original Silicon Valley and the Dallas/Fort Worth area of Texas in the number of high-tech jobs.

More than 10 percent of Colorado's people work in manufacturing jobs in the electronics, scientific instruments, and industrial machinery businesses. Colorado's workers are well educated. The availability of such skilled employees continues to draw more high-tech companies to the state.

Sun Microsystems has built a new research facility in Broomfield, north of Denver. It is expected to employ at least four thousand people. Colorado Springs has an MCI software division as well as the technical center of Federal Express. Integral Peripherals in Boulder is one of the world's largest makers of disk drives for computers. One company in Fort Collins makes the computerized robots that do much of the work in other factories.

The Dinosaur Maker

Chris Mays is an airline pilot who got the idea of using robotics to make dinosaurs in museums come to life. He started Dinamation International Corporation, which makes displays for museums all over the world. He makes certain that all his information on individual dinosaurs is correct by having several paleontologists (scientists who work with fossils) on his staff. In 1994, Mays opened the Devil's Canyon Science and Learning Center in Fruita. It's a place that people can go to learn more about their favorite scientific subjects and see dinosaurs in action. ■

Willing to Gamble

Slot machines in a Central City casino

Coloradans have been willing to gamble since the first adventurers started to pan for gold. In those days, the wide-open mining towns featured gambling in all the saloons, but as "civilized living" took over, gambling was outlawed.

In 1990, Coloradans voted to allow gambling again in certain circumstances to help attract tourists and to bring economic improvements to towns that were on the verge of becoming ghost towns. The following year, casinos opened in Cripple Creek, Central City, and Black Hawk, all within easy access of Denver. Gamblers are limited in the amount they can spend on any single bet so that the state isn't helping people go broke. As on Indian reservations all over the country, the Ute reservations also offer gambling casinos.

Gambling: Pro and Con

The old mining town of Black Hawk was down to three hundred residents when voters approved limited gambling in Colorado. The casino opened in Black Hawk and drew crowds immediately. The money brought into town was used to rescue many beautiful old Victorian houses from deterioration. Serious pollution residues in the countryside from the old mining days were cleaned up. For the first time, the town government now has funds to address the town's needs, such as improving roads and schools.

Not everyone likes the gambling. Thousands of people come into the town every day. Huge parking lots have had to be built. The gamblers disappear after closing time, leaving behind a mess to clean up. The traffic is harming the nearby countryside. Property values have risen so much that old-time residents can no longer afford to live in their hometown. Colorado voters continue to keep an eye on the gambling they voted for.

Agriculture

The High Plains east of Greeley and Fort Collins support a great deal of agriculture. The northeastern corner of the state, watered by the South Platte as it heads into Nebraska, is very productive farmland, featuring sugar beets, hay, and corn. It was this region that Major Stephen Long said would "never be fit for human habitation." The people who took the old Overland Trail through the region must have agreed, because they didn't stop until decades later.

The map of Colorado is very empty south of the South Platte River until the Arkansas River 150 miles (241 km) to the south. Most of the towns in this arid region are along Interstate 70 from Kansas to Denver. Many farmers who are fortunate enough to have irrigation from small rivers have turned to growing sod on their land. Sod is grass that is grown as a crop. A shallow top layer of the ground, grass, roots, and all is removed and rolled up. The rolls of sod are then taken to cities where they are unrolled to make instant lawns.

Harvesting wheat on a Colorado farm

Crop grasses such as hay, winter wheat, and rye take their chances in the arid land between the big rivers. Many years, such crops thrive, but this land between the rivers is the first region to suffer during a drought year.

There are approximately

An Unusual Crop

In the late 1960s, Mo Siegel, a resident of Boulder, went out into the nearby foothills to find herbs, which he dried and sold to health-food stores for herbal teas. Starting with just $800 borrowed from his brother, he built his company, Celestial Seasonings, into one of the biggest tea companies in the world. He is most famous for his Red Zinger tea. Its ingredients include hibiscus, rose hips, and lemongrass. His teas make good reading as well as drinking: the boxes feature beautiful artwork and clever sayings. Today, Celestial Seasonings is owned by Kraft Foods. ■

twenty-five thousand farms in Colorado, each covering an average of about 1,300 acres (526 ha). This average size is quite large compared to the size of farms in most states, but the vast grasslands of the east encourage these large farms.

The San Luis Valley, unlike much of the region, does not have to depend on rivers for its water supply. The valley has artesian wells, which are wells that have water rise in them because of pressure underground. Artesian wells usually do not need pumps to bring the water to the surface. The presence of these artesian wells has allowed the 125-mile (201-km) valley to be turned into an important agricultural area, where a variety of vegetables, especially potatoes, are grown. Some of the moist grassland is also used to raise sheep.

Cattle Country

Almost as soon as Denver became a town, it also became an important cattle center. In 1864, Charles Goodnight and his partner created the Goodnight–Loving Trail from Texas that ended in Denver. The route they chose allowed cowboys to drive cattle to a railhead without going through dangerous Comanche territory.

Author Mari Sandoz wrote in *The Cattlemen:* "Goodnight had planned his drive in the hope that there was some nice money loose for beef in Colorado and certainly there would be grass to hold any stock not readily salable." Charles Goodnight was right. Denver and the area northeast of it became the business center of a huge region of cattle feedlots. Feedlots are fenced areas where cattle that have spent their lives on the open range are taken to be fed for slaughter. In the feedlots, the cattle build up protein in their bodies

Grilled Jalapeño Buffalo Burgers

Exotic meats are popular in Colorado because of their availability and affordability. Buffalo are raised in Colorado for their meat because they are cheaper to feed and require less water than cattle. Since the end of the nineteenth century, buffalo have not only returned from the brink of extinction and flourished in nature preserves, but also are now raised successfully on ranches throughout the West.

Ingredients:

1 lb. ground buffalo
1 medium-sized onion, chopped
1 jalapeño pepper, seeded and chopped
vegetable oil
4 hamburger rolls
Tabasco or other hot sauce

Directions:

Prepare grill.

Mix the buffalo, onion, and pepper together, using your hands. Shape the mixture into four patties.

Brush the grill with vegetable oil to prevent the patties from sticking to it. Grill patties about four or five inches from the coals, turning once. Grill for about four minutes on each side for rare burgers, five to six minutes for medium, and seven minutes for well done. Serve on hamburger rolls with hot sauce.

Serves 4.

that their meat will pass along to people. The object of feedlots used to be to increase the fat content in the meat, but in recent years, people have stopped wanting the white fat, called marbling, that makes meat juicy but not very healthy. Montfort of Colorado is the largest feedlot owner in the nation.

The treeless North, Middle, and South Park areas have been used primarily for grazing cattle and raising hay in recent years. The ranchers used to be able to take their cattle up into open areas

of the surrounding national forests for summer grazing, but very few grazing permits are available anymore. This fact has reduced the number of cattle that most ranches can support. Many ranchers have reluctantly turned their ranches into "dude" ranches. At these tourist spots, visitors ride horses and pretend to be cowboys for a week or so.

Cattle ranches are still a part of Colorado's economy.

Tourism

Today, tourism is the most lucrative part of Colorado's economy. More than 11 million visits by skiers to the twenty-five ski resorts in the state were made in 1997. Although the very fancy resorts where a room can cost $500 a night get most of the publicity, those same resorts, plus many others, also offer winter fun at much lower cost.

Skiers at the base of an Aspen mountain

In a newspaper story about the ski resort of Telluride in the southwestern part of the state, a journalist for the *Chicago Tribune* wrote, "It's old. It's new. It's steep. It's groomed. It's hippies. It's executives. It's remote. It's accessible. It's historic buildings in the town. It's a modern resort on the mountain."

Except for "remote," that description could fit many of the ski resorts in Colorado. In general, they provide many different levels of skiing, and most allow snowboarding, the newest winter fun. In fact, some resorts are

Snowboarding has become popular on Colorado's slopes.

creating special areas especially designed to give the most excitement to snowboarding.

Colorado is not just for winter fun, of course. Its beautiful mountains and its sunshine are just as welcoming in the summer as in the winter.

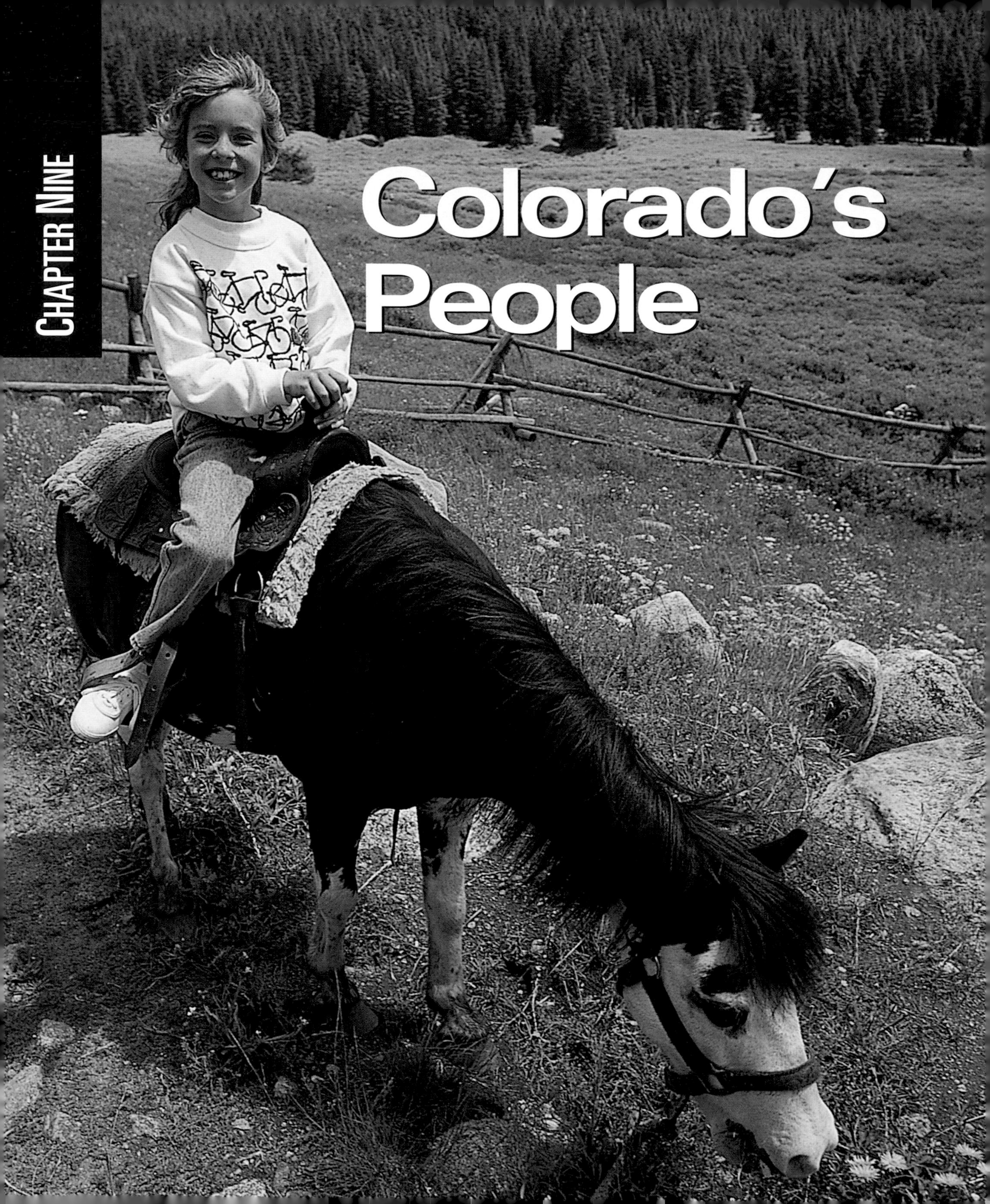

Chapter Nine

Colorado's People

A Ute woman sews a pair of moccasins

Like many states with two or more sections that vary historically and economically, the major sections of Colorado often find it difficult to agree on major issues within the state. East versus West, and Hispanic versus "Anglo" are just two of the divisions.

The percentage of nonwhite people—Latinos, Asian Americans, African-Americans, and Native Americans—is increasing. Much of the reason for this change is that many of the white people who move to Colorado are young and single, looking for good jobs and a sporty way of life. When they do marry, they have few children. On the other hand, most of the nonwhites have lived in the state a long time and are raising large families.

Hispanic Coloradans

The Sangre de Cristo Range was the northern limit of the land once possessed by Mexico. The entire southern region of thirteen counties, especially the San Luis Valley, has remained predominantly Hispanic. The San Luis Valley is known for its prosperous potato farms, but the area as a whole is not very prosperous. Few people have moved there in recent years, and it continues to suffer an economic depression.

Opposite: Horseback riding near Piney Lake

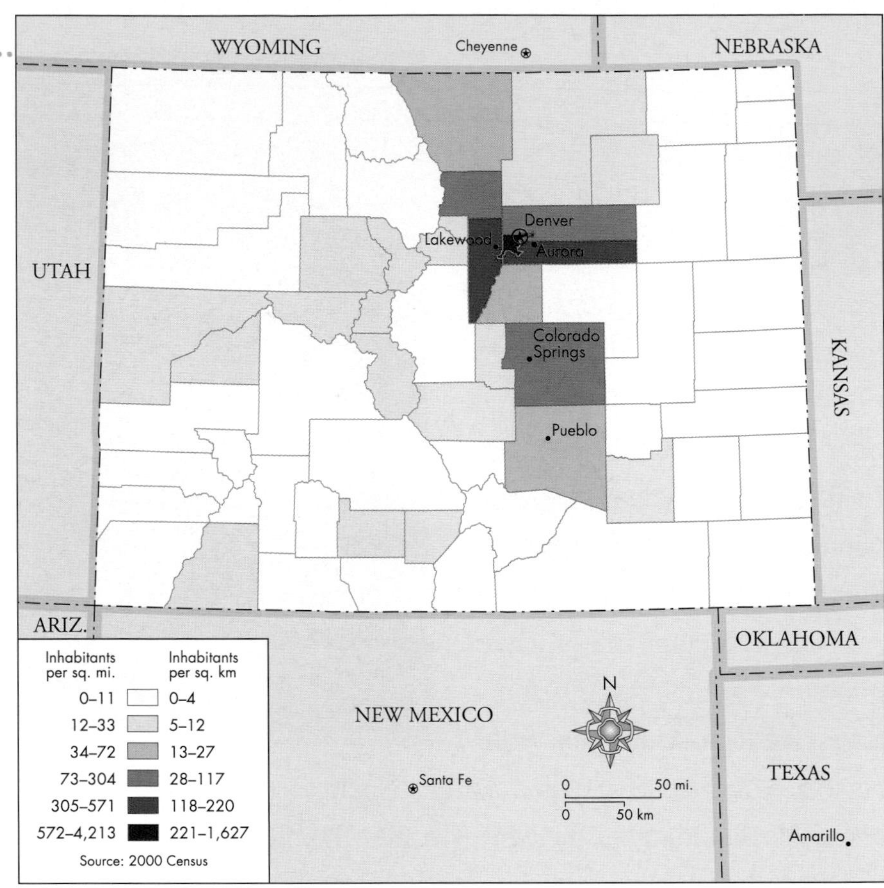

Colorado's population density

The traditional Hispanic regions were augmented during the twentieth century as Hispanics moved in from Mexico. The first large groups were brought in by the steel mills of the Pueblo region. Others were recruited in Mexico to work in the sugar beet fields. The companies that brought in the workers encouraged whole families to come, hoping they would stay. Since then, other Hispanics have moved directly into the farming communities of the eastern rivers. Often, the newcomers have not been allowed to integrate quietly into the communities. As their numbers increased, the Hispanics have often found themselves the target of severe prejudice. Even the old-time Hispanic residents often looked down on the newcomers.

Population of Colorado's Major Cities (2000)

City	Population
Denver	554,636
Colorado Springs	360,890
Aurora	276,393
Lakewood	144,126
Arvada	102,153
Pueblo	102,121

Prominent among Hispanics in the 1960s and 1970s was Rodolfo Gonzales, called "Corky." A native of Denver, he founded the Crusade for Justice to bring together Colorado Hispanics and to give them more control over their lives. Although his organization's political candidates did not pull in many votes, other candidates started paying more attention to the needs of Hispanic voters. Gonzales was more outspoken than many people liked, and in 1973, a member of his organization was killed in an argument with police. Less militant Hispanic leaders gradually took control.

Rodolfo Gonzales tried to unite Colorado Hispanics.

Hispanics make up the largest ethnic group in Colorado. About two-thirds of them have their origins in Mexico. According to the 2000 census, 735,601 Coloradans were Hispanic, a growth of 20 percent since 1990, and Hispanics are expected to make up about 15 percent of the population of Colorado by 2010.

The federal government calculated in 1994 that almost fourteen thousand of Colorado's businesses were owned by Hispanics. Denver has a Hispanic Chamber of Commerce that both encourages Hispanic business and introduces others to what is available in the Hispanic community.

African-Americans

Black men were among the earliest visitors to discover Colorado because many cowboys who herded cattle into and through the region were African-Americans. It's been estimated that perhaps one-fourth of the cattle drivers of the Old West were black.

Paul Stewart, founder of the Black American West Museum and Heritage Center

Paul Stewart, an African-American who has become the foremost historian of black history in the West, started the Black American West Museum and Heritage Center in Denver. It is located in a beautiful Victorian house that was saved from being torn down in 1983.

African-Americans, both former slaves and long free, moved into Colorado after the Civil War. Among them was Frederick Douglass Jr., son of the prominent African-American abolitionist and journalist in the East. He played an influential role in the writing of Colorado's Constitution when the state was preparing to become part of the union. At his urging, the writers included a requirement that the schools not be segregated by race.

However, as in many cities, the public schools of Denver came to be segregated just by the fact that most black people lived in specific areas and the schoolchildren were all black. In 1969, many Denverites tried to establish a busing program that would distribute African-American students into the white schools of the area. When the plan failed to win approval, the backers of the plan went to court. Four years later, the U.S. Supreme Court ruled that Denver must make deliberate efforts to desegregate the schools.

The First Black Resident

The first African-Americans in Colorado were mountain men such as Jim Beckwourth. But a woman was probably the state's first black permanent resident. Clara Brown bought her way out of slavery and was drawn to the mountains of Colorado when rumors of gold started to spread. Though little is known of her early months in the goldfields, she soon built or bought a cabin in the new town of Central City. She turned her home into a boarding house and laundry for miners, and even used it as a hospital on occasion. As the Civil War ended, she used her own funds to bring west to join her members of her family who had been freed from slavery. ■

Public Education

The town of Boulder founded education in Colorado. The miners who worked Gold Hill and built a camp chose in 1860 to build a schoolhouse.

Today, Colorado children are required to attend school from age seven to age sixteen. In recent decades, the nature of the schools they attend has changed for many children. Many parents were not happy with the way the public schools were run and the subjects that children were taught. Two newer kinds of schooling have become very popular. Children in home schooling are taught by one or

several parents who have demonstrated to officials that they are qualified to teach. Several home schools often work together to hold field trips and sports activities, so that children do not learn in isolation.

The General Assembly approved the idea of charter schools in 1993. Charter schools are privately operated but funded with money from the school district. The idea has become very popular. Most charter schools emphasize the subjects considered core knowledge—"reading, writing, and 'rithmetic."

A high school class in Durango

Home schooling and charter schools, however, do not solve Colorado's problems with public education. The number of young people who drop out at sixteen, especially Hispanic young people, is far too high. Also, the quality of education in a state that depends on a large number of well-educated technological employees has become inadequate.

Colorado businesspeople are working to relieve some of the state's education problems with at least two programs. In a statewide program, schools and businesses have formed a School-to-Career Partnership. Both educators and business leaders are trying to ensure that Colorado's students graduate with the skills needed to build a career. In addition, on a more local level, individual businesses participate in the Adopt-a-School program, in which businesspeople help individual schools achieve their goals with their students.

A charter school in Pueblo

Higher Education

Settlement in Colorado was less than six years old when the first institution of higher education was established. In 1864, John Evans, the governor of Colorado Territory, started the Colorado Seminary for the Methodist Episcopal Church. It soon had to close its doors, but it reopened in 1880 as the University of Denver. Evans had already founded Northwestern University and the city of Evanston, just north of Chicago.

Boulder has been famous for education ever since it opened Colorado's first school. Only a year later, in 1861, the groundwork was laid for the University of Colorado, though it did not actually open its doors until 1876. The United States' only Buddhist university, called Naropa Institute, is just one of several schools of higher education located in Boulder.

M. Scott Carpenter, one of the original seven American astronauts (and the only one who also became an aquanaut for NASA),

From a Mining Camp

Florence Rena Sabin was born in 1871 in Central City, where her father was a mining engineer. When she was seven, her mother died, and her father sent Florence and her sister to live with relatives in Chicago. After high school, she was accepted at Johns Hopkins University, one of the most prestigious medical schools in the nation. She later became the first woman to hold the rank of full professor at Johns Hopkins. Sabin was also instrumental in getting important health and sanitation laws passed in Colorado. In 1925, Sabin was the first woman to be named to the National Academy of Sciences. This organization, which has a limited membership, recognizes achievements in science. Colorado also recognized Sabin—a statue of her as one of Colorado's most illustrious residents is in Statuary Hall at the U.S. Capitol in Washington, D.C. ■

is a native of Boulder. Edward Condon of the University of Colorado was head of the famed Bluebook Project for the U.S. Air Force in the 1960s. Bluebook was the official investigation into reports of unidentified flying objects, or UFOs.

Astronaut M. Scott Carpenter is a native of Boulder.

The National Center for Atmospheric Research was built on a mesa near Boulder. The center is affiliated with fifty universities and does work for them that no one university could manage to do on its own. For example, its amazing computer system can handle the measurements being input from more than two thousand locations around the globe.

Among the other universities in Colorado are the University of Southern Colorado at Pueblo, University of Northern Colorado at Greeley, and Western State College of Colorado at Gunnison.

Air Pollution

Coloradans—as well as visitors—began to realize in the 1960s that while there may have been wonderful mountains near Denver, they weren't able to see them very well. The air quality in the capital city had become so bad from all the traffic that there was no longer something called "pure mountain air" in the nearby mountains.

Colorado was not alone with this problem, and in 1970, the U.S. Congress passed the Clean Air Act to establish national policy. Colorado started a state government agency called Clean Air Colorado charged with the responsibility of keeping air pollution to a

Whizzer White

Byron (called "Whizzer") White (1917–) of the University of Colorado was one of the great college football stars of the 1930s and 1940s. Born at Fort Collins, he was named All-American when he played halfback at the university. In 1954, he was named to the National Football Hall of Fame. Eight years later in 1962, President John F. Kennedy named Whizzer White to the U.S. Supreme Court. White left the bench in 1993. ■

A cloud of pollution hanging over Denver

minimum. Over the years, the mountains have become visible again. When pollution levels are high (which tends to be during the winter months), however, Denver residents are not allowed to burn wood in their fireplaces. They are also encouraged to use public transportation systems to help limit automobile exhaust fumes in the area.

Denver is not alone with the pollution problem. Some of the beautiful resort areas are located in valleys where pollution builds up when traffic on the narrow, congested roads is particularly bad. State highway officials are working to develop plans for roads and tunnels that will help eliminate such air pollution.

Dealing with Wildlife

As residents of a "frontier" state, Coloradans have to deal with wildlife more than people do in many other states. There are still plenty of black bears and mountain lions in the mountains, and they often venture down into the suburbs of major cities.

In many towns, the residents are required to have bear-proof trash cans so that their garbage won't attract animals. Schools on the edge of wild areas give children lessons in what to do if they run into one of the large mammals.

Coloradans must make up their minds whether they are in favor of population growth or trying to preserve the wilderness that drew them to the state in the first place. In 1951, when people needed to be encouraged to move to the state, the legislature passed a law guaranteeing that if a bear or a wild cat damaged a homestead, or fence, or other property, the state would pay the costs of repairs. That scheme worked all right when there were only a few isolated cabins or ranches out in the wilderness. Now, however, whole housing developments are being built where wild animals still roam. Many people recognize that the government can't keep on paying such costs.

Some of Colorado's bears rummage through garbage cans.

Residents disagree on what should be done. Some old-time residents think that newcomers should be required to sign an agreement stating that they understand they are moving into an area populated by wildlife. This would relieve the state government of any liability for damages incurred by wild animals. The state—which has spent a lot of money to attract people to Colorado—disagrees. The discussion will probably continue until there are so few large wild animals left that there is no longer a problem.

Chapter Ten

Of Snow, Sports, and Songs

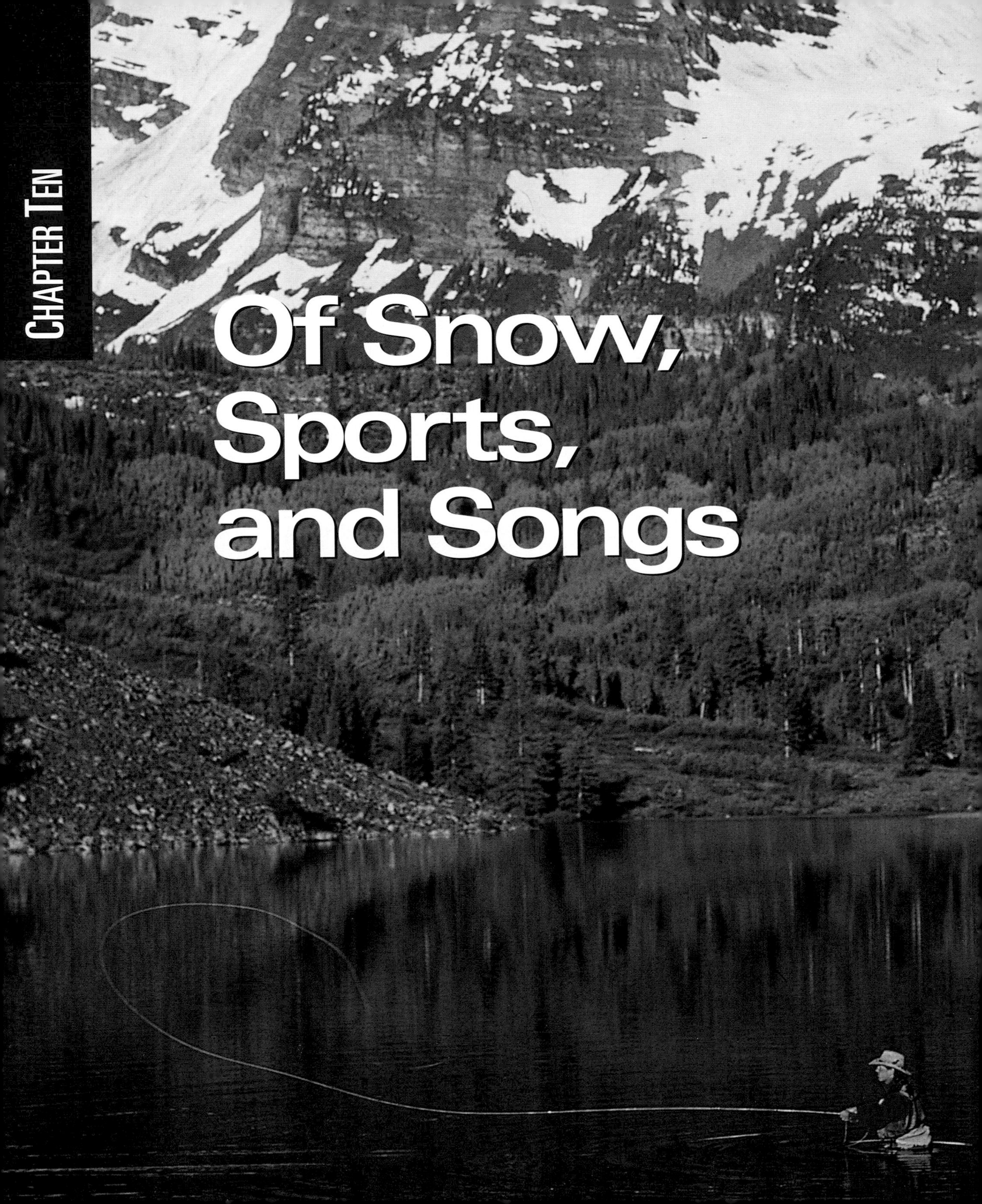

Downhill skiing is one of Colorado's main attractions.

The snow of the Colorado Rockies is the focus of much sports activity in the state. Its location in the center of the country draws people from north, east, south, and west to ski. The beautiful scenery, as well, draws people year-round.

As early as 1870, people left the security of their towns and cities to enjoy "roughing it" in the mountains of Colorado. Even ladies in their long dresses enjoyed getting out into the wilderness and camping on a mountainside. The mountains continue to provide the ideal setting for hiking, camping, climbing, trout fishing, white-water rafting, and studying mountain plants and animals.

Skiing

People from Norway and Sweden who came to work in the mines probably first brought skiing to Colorado. The sport became a feature of the luxury hotels, such as the Broadmoor in Colorado Springs, early in the twentieth century.

Today, there are more than two dozen ski areas in Colorado. Most of them have ski lifts that can carry skiers to the top of the long groomed runs on the mountains. They also offer cross-country skiing, in which people ski along planned trails through forests and down smaller hills.

Aspen and Vail are called "world-class" ski resorts. They are

Opposite: Fly fishing in Maroon Lake

Cross-country skiing is also offered at the resorts.

The Manassa Mauler

Manassa is a small town in the San Luis Valley where, in 1895, William Harrison Dempsey was born, one of eleven children. Before he was even past his teens, the boy, who called himself Jack Dempsey, made a name for himself by winning fights staged in the mining camps of Colorado. It was there he earned the name "The Manassa Mauler." Dempsey reached the top in 1919, when he won the world heavyweight boxing title from Jess Willard. He defended his title several times, finally losing it to Gene Tunney in 1926. ■

equivalent to the famous older ski facilities in the Alps of Europe, and, like European ski areas, they draw people from all over the world. In 1989, the World Alpine Ski Championships, the biggest contest in skiing, was held in Vail. It was only the second time this major ski event was held in the United States.

Some of the other ski areas, such as those of Summit County, are reaching world-class status. Because Summit is so close to Denver (only about 70 miles, or 113 km), it draws considerably more people for a wider variety of sports. Arapahoe Basin in Summit County is one of the oldest skiing areas in Colorado.

Colorado's great skiing attracted the International Olympic Committee, and Denver was chosen as the site of the 1976 Winter Olympics. Costs to prepare for the big event escalated, though, and in 1972, opposition to holding the Olympics increased. Enough people opposed the expense—and possible environmental damage—to put the issue on the November ballot. Voters rejected the Olympics. Instead, they were held in 1976 in Innsbruck, Austria, which had held the games twelve years before and still had most facilities available.

Five years after Coloradans rejected the plan to hold the 1976 Winter Olympics in the Denver area, the official U.S. Olympics Training Center opened in Colorado Springs. Up to six hundred athletes in any of a variety of sports can live and train at the facility at one time. In addition, the national headquarters of the governing bodies for nine different Olympic sports are located at or near the facility.

"Totally Cool" Snowboarding

The fairly new sport called snowboarding is the wintertime equivalent of skateboarding. Both feet fit in braces on a single board, instead of the traditional two boards of skiing. The snowboarder can do flips and other tricks like a skateboarder, tricks that the skier can't do.

The World Snowboarding Championships are held in Breckenridge.

Although skiers used to regard the moguls (bumps) in the ski trail as a nuisance, nowadays, bumpy snow-covered hills draw snowboarders by the thousands. Many snowboarding areas have also constructed half-pipes, which are banks of hard-packed snow with a smooth area in between them. Snowboarders can ride them up and down the way skateboarders ride ramps. Snowboarding was described by one Colorado youngster as "totally, totally cool!"

The world's first snowboarding competition was held in Leadville in 1981. Five years later, the World Snowboarding Championships, which had started in 1983 in Lake Tahoe, were permanently moved to Breckenridge. They are held every March. Many ski hills in

Colorado did not allow snowboarders to use their ski runs, however, considering snowboarding too "rambunctious." Gradually, though, the owners of ski hills realized that more and more people wanted to snowboard, and if they couldn't do it in Colorado, they would go elsewhere. In 1989, Vail opened its hills to snowboarders; in 1996, Aspen concurred.

Olympics competition wasn't far behind. The 1998 Winter Olympics, held in Nagano, Japan, included snowboarding as an official winter Olympic sport for the first time. The snow-grooming machine used in those Winter Olympics in Japan was the Pipe Dragon, invented by Doug Waugh, a Colorado farmer.

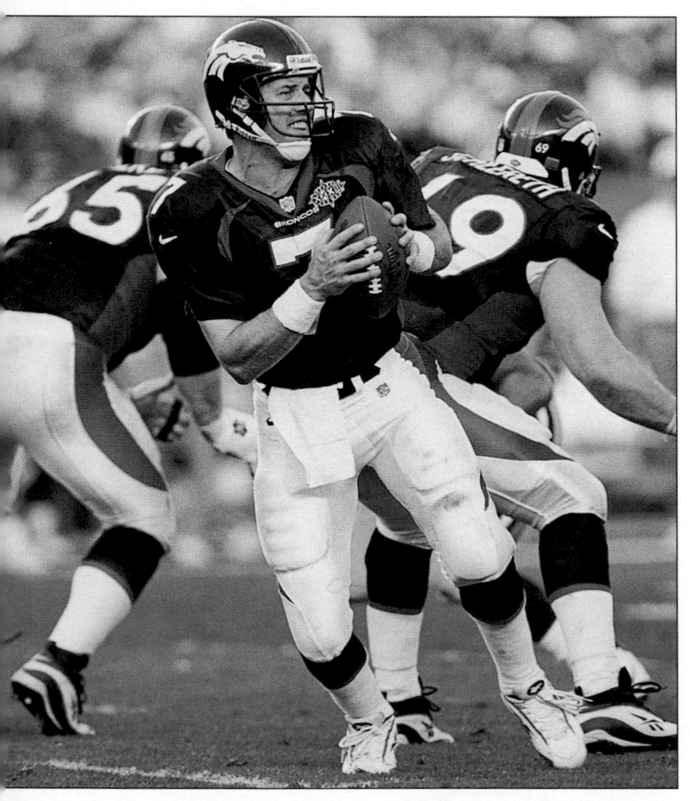

John Elway led the Denver Broncos to a 1998 Super Bowl victory.

The Broncos

The Denver Broncos professional football team was started in 1960. It was everybody's favorite underdog until 1998. The team—named for the untamed horses of the West—had made it to the Super Bowl (the National Football League championship game) four times and lost each time (in 1978, 1987, 1988, and 1990).

Denver fans despaired of ever coming out on top, but 1998 proved a magical year. Playing the highly favored Green Bay Packers, Denver pulled off an upset and won their first Super Bowl championship. For Bronco legend John Elway, the game was the crowning achievement of the great quarterback's career.

The Broncos belong to the Western Division of the American Football Conference. They play at Denver's Mile-High Stadium, which was built in 1948 and holds 76,000 fans. In 1998, voters in the six counties of the Denver area agreed to have their sales taxes increased to pay for a new Mile-High Stadium for the Broncos. The team trains on the fields of the University of Northern Colorado at Greeley.

Other Professional Teams

Denver, with the help of Coors Brewery (which has the world's largest single beer-brewing facility in Golden) built an important new ballpark, with the feel of an old-time park. It is now the home of the Colorado Rockies of the National League. The Rockies team was added to the lineup of the National League as an expansion team in 1993. Just three years later, the Rockies made the playoffs, becoming the only baseball expansion team to reach the post-season in less than eight years. Playing at Coors Field can be heaven if you're a home-run hitter but a nightmare for pitchers. In the thin mountain air, home runs fly out of the park, and Denver fans see very few low-scoring games.

The Denver Nuggets professional basketball team plays in the Midwest Division of the Western Conference. They

The Colorado Rockies play in baseball's National League.

were division champs in 1977 and 1978, as well as 1985 and 1988. The Nuggets play in the McNichols Sports Arena in Denver. Built in 1975, it holds more than 17,000 fans.

Denver's professional ice hockey team is the Colorado Avalanche. Originally from Canada, the team moved to Denver in 1979. It won the 1996 Stanley Cup.

Professional soccer came to Denver in 1996, with the formation of Major League Soccer (MLS). The Colorado Rapids team plays in the Western Conference of the MLS.

College Teams

The two biggest college teams in the state play their football and basketball games in separate leagues. The University of Colorado Buffaloes play in the Big Twelve Conference. The Colorado State Rams play in the Western Athletic Conference.

There is no final playoff that determines the college football champions each year, but since 1936, sportswriters have made an unofficial selection to which fans pay attention. In 1990, the Colorado Buffaloes tied with Georgia Tech in the selection. In 1994, Colorado's Rashaan Salaam won the Heisman Trophy, the nation's top award to a college football player.

Colorado Performance

Colorado towns and cities draw many visitors, and most of them hold arts festivals of various kinds. Aspen, for example, holds a summer-long music festival. The beautiful old opera houses in Central City and Leadville are still used for live entertainment.

Red Rocks Amphitheater, located near Morrison, west of

Denver, is a natural bowl that has been turned into an outdoor theater where cultural events are held during the summer. The bowl is surrounded by Colorado's famed red sandstone monoliths that enhance the sunset the audience enjoys as they listen to music.

Broadway theater actress and director Antoinette Perry was born in Denver, granddaughter of a gold-rush miner. Throughout her career, she was an avid supporter of American theater and its actors and actresses. After her death in 1946, the theater equivalent of Hollywood's Oscars was named the Tony after Antoinette Perry.

The Grateful Dead is one of many groups who have appeared at Red Rocks Amphitheater.

Music Makers

One of the greatest musical names associated with Colorado is the late John Denver. Born Henry John Deutschendorf in New Mexico, he changed his name to Denver and became one of the greatest spokespeople for Colorado. A resident of Aspen, he invited others to share his love of the mountains with such songs as "Rocky Mountain High," which many Coloradans hope to make the state song. Denver, a pilot, died in a small plane accident in California in 1997.

Singer/songwriter John Denver made Colorado his home.

Timeline

United States History

1607 The first permanent British settlement is established in North America at Jamestown.

1620 Pilgrims found Plymouth Colony, the second permanent British settlement.

1776 America declares its independence from England.

1783 The Treaty of Paris officially ends the Revolutionary War in America.

1787 The U.S. Constitution is written.

1803 Louisiana Purchase almost doubles the size of the United States.

1812–15 United States and Britain fight the War of 1812.

1861–65 The North and South fight each other in the American Civil War.

Colorado State History

1706 Juan de Ulibarri and his soldiers explore the region centered around what is now the city of Pueblo.

1779 Juan Bautista de Anza gathers Utes to fight with his army against the Comanche.

1806 Zebulon Pike leads an expedition into Colorado and gets his first sight of the Rocky Mountains.

1846 The area north of the Rio Grande (including Colorado) is ceded to the United States by Mexico.

1858 Gold prospectors pan for gold in Cherry Creek.

1861 Colorado Territory is established by the federal government in February.

1876 Colorado is admitted to the United States as the thirty-eighth state.

1891 The discovery of gold at Cripple Creek turns the area into the largest U.S. gold producer for several years.

United States History

1917–18 The United States is involved in World War I.

1929 The Stock market crashes, plunging the United States into the Great Depression.

1941–45 The United States fights in World War II.

1945 The United States becomes a charter member of the U.N.

1951–53 The United States fights in the Korean War.

1964 The U.S. Congress enacts a series of groundbreaking civil rights laws.

1964–73 The United States engages in the Vietnam War.

1991 The United States and other nations fight the brief Persian Gulf War against Iraq.

Colorado State History

1923 Benjamin F. Stapleton is elected mayor of Denver.

1927 The Moffat Tunnel is opened.

1958 The U.S. Air Force Academy opens its campus near Colorado Springs.

1966 The North American Aerospace Defense Command (NORAD) completes its underground center in Cheyenne Mountain.

1973 The Eisenhower–Johnson Memorial Tunnel, the world's highest road tunnel, is completed.

1983 Federico Peña becomes Denver's first Hispanic mayor.

1993 The Colorado Rockies begin playing Major League Baseball in Denver.

1995 Denver International Airport opens.

Fast Facts

Colorado's state capital building in Denver

Rocky Mountain columbine

Statehood date	August 1, 1876, the 38th state
Origin of state name	From a Spanish word meaning "red-colored," first used to describe the Colorado River
State capital	Denver
State nickname	Centennial State
State motto	*Nil sine Numine* (Nothing without Providence)
State bird	Lark bunting
State flower	Rocky Mountain columbine
State song	"Where the Columbines Grow"
State tree	Colorado blue spruce
State animal	Rocky Mountain bighorn sheep
State fish	Greenback cutthroat trout
State folk dance	Square dance
State fossil	Stegosaurus
State grass	Blue grama grass
State gemstone	Aquamarine
State insect	Colorado hairstreak butterfly
State fair	Pueblo (August)

Rocky Mountain bighorn sheep

Total area; rank	104,100 sq. mi. (269,618 sq km), 8th
Land area; rank	103,729 sq. mi. (268,657 sq km), 8th
Water area; rank	371 sq. mi. (960 sq km), 43rd
***Inland water;* rank**	371 sq. mi. (960 sq km), 38th
Geographic center	Park, 30 miles (48 km) northwest of Pikes Peak
Latitude and longitude	Colorado is located approximately between 37° 00′ and 41° 00′ N and 102° 03′ and 109° 03′ W
Highest point	Mount Elbert, 14,433 feet (4,399 m)
Lowest point	Along the Arkansas River in Prowers County, 3,350 feet (1,021 m)
Largest city	Denver
Number of counties	63
Longest river	Colorado
Population; rank	4,301,261 (2000 census); 24th
Density	41 persons per sq. mi. (16 per sq km)
Population distribution	82% urban, 18% rural
Ethnic distribution (does not equal 100%)	White 82.8% Hispanic 17.1% Other 7.2% African-American 3.8% Asian and Pacific Islanders 2.2% Native American 1.0%
Record high temperature	118°F (48°C) at Bennett on July 11, 1888

Denver skyline

High school students

Record low temperature	-61°F (-52°C) at Maybell in Moffat County on February 1, 1985
Average July temperature	74°F (23°C)
Average January temperature	28°F (-2°C)
Average annual precipitation	15 inches (38 cm)

Colorado's Natural Areas

National Parks

Black Canyon of the Gunnison National Park is a sheer-walled canyon with geologically interesting ancient rocks.

Mesa Verde National Park contains pre-Columbian cliff dwellings and other relics of early people.

Rocky Mountain National Park sits along the Continental Divide.

National Historic Site

Bent's Old Fort National Historic Site is a frontier trading post along the Santa Fe Trail.

Mesa Verde National Park

National Monuments

Colorado National Monument contains canyons, dinosaur fossils, and remains of prehistoric Native American cultures.

Dinosaur National Monument contains a quarry with dinosaur and other ancient animal fossils.

Florissant Fossil Beds National Monument preserves the fossil remains of ancient insects, seeds, and leaves, as well as petrified tree stumps.

Great Sand Dunes National Monument contains some of the largest and tallest sand dunes in the United States.

Black Canyon of the Gunnison River

Hovenweep National Monument is made up of six groups of towers, cliff dwellings, and pueblos built by Native Americans.

National Recreation Area

Curecanti National Recreation Area is made up of Blue Mesa, Crystal, and Morrow Point Lakes.

Sports Teams

NCAA Teams (Division I)

Colorado State University Rams

U.S. Air Force Academy Falcons

University of Colorado Buffaloes

Major League Soccer

Colorado Rapids

Major League Baseball

Colorado Rockies

National Basketball Association

Denver Nuggets

National Football Association

Denver Broncos

National Hockey League

Colorado Avalanche

Denver Broncos

Cultural Institutions

Libraries

Denver Public Library is the oldest library in the state.

State Historical Society of Colorado (Denver) contains interesting historical documents on the early days of Colorado.

Libraries of the University of Colorado (Boulder) contain a fine collection of Mexicana and other books on early Americana.

The Red Rocks Amphitheater

Museums

Black American West Museum and Heritage Center (Denver)

Colorado History Museum (Denver)

Denver Museum of Natural History

Denver Art Museum

Boulder Museum of History chronicles the settlement and industrial development of Boulder.

Performing Arts

Colorado has three major opera companies, two major symphony orchestras, one major dance company, and one major professional theater company.

Universities and Colleges

In the mid-1990s, Colorado had twenty-eight public and thirty-one private institutions of higher education.

Annual Events

January–March

National Western Stock Show in Denver (January)

Breckenridge Ullrfest Winter Carnival (January)

Steamboat Springs Winter Carnival (February)

World Cup Ski Racing Competitions in Vail and Aspen (February and March)

World Snowboarding Championships in Breckenridge (March)

Winter Park Wingbreak (April)

April–June

Iron Horse Bicycle Classic in Durango (May)

Telluride Wine Festival (June)

Telluride Bluegrass Festival (June)

Frog Rodeo in Empire (June)

July–September

Denver Cherry Creek Arts Festival (July)

Strings in the Mountains Chamber Music Festival in Steamboat Springs (July)

Central City Opera Festival (July and August)

Colorado Shakespeare Festival in Boulder (July and August)

Festival of the Arts in Crested Butte (August)

Colorado State Fair in Pueblo (August)

Festival of Mountain and Plain in Denver (September)

Larimer Square Oktoberfest in Denver (September)

October–December

Parade of Lights in Denver (December)

Famous People

Katharine Lee Bates (1859–1929)	Author and educator
James Pierson (Jim) Beckwourth (1798–1867?)	Frontiersman and scout
Albert Bierstadt (1830–1902)	Landscape painter
Black Kettle (?–1868)	Cheyenne chief
Margaret Tobin (Molly) Brown (1873–1932)	Pioneer and *Titanic* survivor
M. Scott Carpenter (1925–)	Astronaut
George Catlin (1796–1872)	Artist and author
Lon Chaney (1883–1930)	Actor
William Harrison (Jack) Dempsey (1895–1983)	Boxer
Zebulon Montgomery Pike (1779–1813)	Army officer and explorer
Byron Raymond White (1917–)	Supreme Court justice
Darryl F. Zanuck (1902–1979)	Movie producer

M. Scott Carpenter

To Find Out More

History

- Bledsoe, Sara. *Colorado.* Minneapolis: Lerner, 1993.
- Fradin, Dennis Brindell. *Colorado.* Chicago: Childrens Press, 1993.
- Lawlor, Laurie. *Gold in the Hills.* New York: Walker & Co, 1995.
- Liggett, Diane T., and James A. Mack. *Real Cool Colorado Places for Curious Kids.* Englewood, Colo.: Westcliffe Publishing, 1998.
- Thompson, Kathleen. *Colorado.* Austin, Tex.: Raintree/Steck Vaughn, 1996.
- Wills, Charles A. *A Historical Album of Colorado.* Brookfield, Conn.: Millbrook Press, 1996.

Fiction

- Hobbs, Will. *Beardance.* New York: Atheneum, 1993.
- Myers, Edward P. *Climb or Die.* New York: Hyperion Press, 1997.

Biographies

- Campbell, Robin. *Florence Sabin: Scientist.* Broomall, Penn.: Chelsea House, 1996.
- Epstein, Vivian Sheldon. *History of Colorado's Women for Young People.* Denver: Vivian Sheldon Epstein Publishers, 1997.
- Fraser, Mary Ann. *In Search of the Grand Canyon/Down the Colorado with John Wesley Powell.* New York: Henry Holt & Company, Inc., 1995.

Websites

- **State of Colorado Home-page**
  http://www.state.co.us/
  The official homepage for the state of Colorado

- **Colorado State Archives**
  http://www.state.co.us/gov_dir/gss/archives/index.html
  Complete historical and governmental information about Colorado

Addresses

- **Colorado Tourism Board**
  1625 Broadway
  Suite 1700
  Denver, CO 80202
  For information on travel and tourism in Colorado

- **Legislative Council**
  State Capitol Building
  Denver, CO 80203
  For information about Colorado's government

- **Colorado Historical Society**
  1300 Broadway
  Denver, CO 80203
  For information about Colorado's history

Index

Page numbers in *italics* indicate illustrations.

Meet the Author

Jean Blashfield's first trip to Colorado was to attend an aerospace education conference. During that trip she got to set off model rockets against a backdrop of blue skies and magnificent mountains, and she never quite recovered.

During many years in publishing, including developing the classic *Young People's Science Encyclopedia* for Children's Press, she lived in Chicago; London, England; and Washington, D.C. But when she married Wallace Black (a Chicago publisher, writer, and pilot), they chose Colorado for their honeymoon. Since then, she's been back several times and has always found the state enchanting. Today, she has two college-age children, three cats, and two computers in her Victorian home in Delavan, Wisconsin.

Jean Blashfield has written about eighty books, most of them for young people. She likes best to write about interesting places, but she loves history and science, too. In fact, one of her big advantages as a writer is that she becomes fascinated by just about every subject she investigates. She has created an encyclopedia of aviation and space, written popular books on murderers and house plants, and had a lot of fun creating an early book on the things women have done, called *Hellraisers, Heroines, and Holy Women.*

She and Wally later formed their own company, which took advantage of Jean's massive collection of 3 x 5 cards. The cards contained interesting tidbits of information about many states, their places and people. Today, she has all that research on computer. In fact, she uses computers to broaden her research on Colorado and many other subjects. She also produces whole books on the computer—scanning pictures, creating layouts, and even developing the index. She has become an avid Internet surfer and is working on her own website, but she'll never give up her trips to the library.

She has written several America the Beautiful books for Children's Press and has been particularly pleased to be able to write this book, on the state where "America the Beautiful" was written.

Photo Credits

Photographs ©:

Allsport USA: 123 (Mike Powell), 124, 133 bottom (Rick Stewart)
AP/Wide World Photos: 91 (John Duricka)
Ben Klaffke: 6 top left, 8, 54, 64, 70, 108 top
Bob Clemenz Photography: 48 (Bob & Suzanne Clemenz)
Branson Reynolds: 10, 12, 55, 79, 111, 115 top, 132 top
Brown Brothers: 9
Celestial Seasonings: 106 (Golin/Harris)
Colorado Historical Society: 71 (Gwenyth D. Goldsberry), 36
Corbis-Bettmann: 96 (Reuters), 57, 113 top, 118 (UPI), 40 (Baldwin H. Ward), 21, 25, 31, 116
Culver Pictures: 23, 29, 32, 39
Denver Public Library, Western History Department: 37 (Harry Rhoads), 17, 22, 28, 30, 33, 35, 38, 41
Envision: 107 (Peter Johansky)
H. Armstrong Roberts, Inc.: cover (H. Abernathy), 72 (J. Blank), 95 (P. Degginger)
Monkmeyer Press: 74 (Das)
NASA: 117, 135
National Geographic Image Collection: 102 (Brooks Walker)
Network Aspen: 7 top left, 75, 80, 90 bottom, 108 bottom, 121 (Jeffrey Aaronson), 105 (David Lissy), 6 bottom, 109, 127 (John Russell)
North Wind Picture Archives: 14, 15, 20, 34
O'hara Photography: 113 bottom (Sherri Stewart O'Hara)
Photo Researchers: 119 (Alan D. Carey), back cover (Jeff Greenberg), 92, 132 bottom (Richard Hutchings), 86, 130 bottom (Jeff Lepore), 99 (Mark D. Phillips), 7 bottom, 59, 131 top (Len Rue Jr.), 98 (Stephen Saks), 49 (Gilda Schiff)
Photographers/Aspen, Inc.: 120 (Brian Bailey), 43 (Paul Chesley), 63 (Tony Demin), 126, 134 (Michael Lewis)
Richardson Photography: 46, 58, 76, 125 (Jim Richardson)
Stock Montage, Inc.: 18
The Denver Post: 90 top, 100, 115 bottom (Steve Nehf)
Tom Stack & Associates: 82, 130 top (David L. Brown), 104 (Ann Duncan), 7 top right, 110 (Brian Parker), 56, 133 top (Doug Sokell), 67, 78 (Spencer Swanger)
Tony Stone Images: 6 top right, 62 (Glen Allison), 42 (Paul Chesley), 73 (Barbara Filet), 122 (David Hiser), 7 top center, 83, 131 bottom (Richard Kaylin), 2 (James Randklev), 97 (Bob Thomason), 94 (Randy Wells), 61
Visuals Unlimited: 53 (Patricia K. Armstrong), 6 top center, 44 (Bill Banaszewski), 51 (B. J. Barton), 66, 69 (Mark E. Gibson), 65, 68 (Jeff Greenberg)
Maps by XNR Productions, Inc.